THE BOOK on INTERNAL STRESS RELEASE

Coach Melvin with Lineage Master Bruce Frantzis, from whom he learned Opening the Energy Gates of Your Body, the Qigong energetic meditation which the popular Coach bases his tradmarked, Dynamic Application of Internal Awareness (DAIA) Method on. Master Frantzis is included among the many Preeminent Qigong / Tai Chi Chuan adepts listed in this publication.

THE BOOK on INTERNAL STRESS RELEASE

Get Powerful Health and Nutritional Secrets

R. Melvin "Coach Melvin" McKenzie

with

Dr. John P. Painter and Dr. Carl A. Totton

Published by
CreateSpace

Copyright © 2015 R. Melvin McKenzie
All rights reserved

Published by CreateSpace
100 Enterprise Way
Suite A200
Scotts Valley, CA 95066
Phone: 1-206-922-0860

No part of this publication may be reproduced, stored in a retrieval system, or transmitted, in any form, or by any means, electronic, mechanical, photocopying, recording, or otherwise, without the prior consent of the publisher.

The publisher makes no representations or warranties with respect to the accuracy or completeness of the contents of this book and specifically disclaims any implied warranties of merchantability or fitness for a particular purpose. Neither the publisher nor authors shall be liable for any loss of profit or any commercial damages.

The Book on Internal STRESS Release: Get Powerful Health and Nutritional Secrets, is sponsored by KEH Marketing, a subsidiary of Kanda Equity Holdings, LLC, an asset management firm. The mission of the firm is to help you live a nutritionally and financially healthy lifestyle.

If you have any type of medical condition restricting your ability to engage in physical

activity, it is suggested you consult your medical physician before attempting any mental or

physical techniques within this publication, or utilizing any of the nutritional methods given.

This information is not intended as a substitute for professional medical advice or treatme

Paperback Revision

CreateSpace
ISBN-13: 978-1519557681
ISBN-10: 151955768X

Library of Congress Control Number: 2015919839

BISAC: Body, Mind & Spirit / Meditation / Health & Fitnes

The Book on Internal STRESS Release: Get Powerful Health and Nutritional Secrets is dedicated to you. It is not by chance you chose to read this; you were destined to to be richly rewarded, beginning today, with exceptional health and overflowing wealth. This is your vehicle.

൞

Acknowledgements

I acknowledge the One whom is my center and circumference—Jesus Christ. He gives me the breath of life, radiant health, and abundant blessings.

Several high-level internal martial arts teachers introduced me to the concept of nei gung, which is loosely translated as "*chi*": Dr. Chiang Yun-Chung, my first internal martial arts teacher, followed in succession by Dr. Zhou Ting-Jue; Jiang Hao-Quan; Liang Qiang-Ya; Dr. Bruce Frantzis, and John Bracy. However, I must give credit to Dr. Frantzis, who personally taught me to realize, develop, and mentally control the internal energy within my body.

My book coach, Raymond Aaron, the nation's number #1 success and investment coach and New York Times Top Ten Bestselling Author, was key to the publication and success of my award-winning publication, The Book on Amazing, Internal **STRESS** Release: 10 Steps to Free Yourself Forever, from which this revised book was derived. Thanks to Dr. John Gray, New York Times #1 Best-Selling Author, who was present at my award ceremony, and, to Debbi Dachinger, award-winning syndicated radio host, International Bestseller, and Success and Media Expert, for their kind, unselfish endorsements.

Special thanks to **Jack M. Zufelt**, author of the best selling book, The DNA of Success which hit the #1 bestseller slot in the first 3 weeks it was out. It is now in 15 languages. His exceptional wisdom and foresight has added great value to this publication.

May God put His blessings on this work, allowing it to be of benefit to all whom reads it.

GIFTS FROM THE COACH

The Book on Internal STRESS Release: Get Powerful Health and Nutritional Secrets, **rewards you further with two included gifts. Actually, these gifts establish the validity of this book.**

Gift #1 - NEVER PAY FULL RETAIL again on healthy, natural and organic food products. Coach Melvin believes everyone should have access to such food sources that does what nature intended: provide unhindered nutrition to the body for its livelihood, healing and rejuvenation. **Here is FREE** access to thousands of healthy, products up to 50% off, including free delivery to your door - **www.More.sh/Organic-Healthfood**

Ditching junk food and switching to the healthier choice doesn't have to be a financial pain. In fact, you can actually save both time and money when you make a handful of simple swaps. It's simple & easy for members on a budget to stay healthy. Whether you're hunting for safe sunscreen, or looking to satisfy your sweet-tooth minus refined sugar, they have the highest-quality non-GMO products you love at the lowest possible prices.

Gift #2 - MUSIC IS AN EXCELLENT STRESS RELEASER - Now you can learn to play piano from a **computer song tutor!** FREE action video and software demonstration! **www.More.sh/Computer-SongTutor**

Even if you've never, **EVER** touched a piano keyboard or synthesizer during your whole lifetime, this free pesentation shows you how a computer song tutor can teach you anything you ever wanted to know about music. You can actually start playing your favorite songs **within minutes** with a new revolutionary tool never shared with the public...*UNTIL NOW!* Discover secrets even most musicians will never know about playing by ear. Learn any song by understanding one thing: like how to use just 4 chords and a handful of patterns to play any song you want!

Visit the link above if you've ever wanted to fulfill a life-long dream of learning piano, or any other instruments by ear, **without reading sheet music**.

Special Bonus – List of Preeminent Qigong / Tai Chi Chuan masters. Included within this publication.

This is a special bonus featuring an A-list of *highly* skilled Qigong and Internal Martial Arts masters. These esteemed professionals—some of them highly qualified MDs, NDs, DOs, O.M.Ds, herbologists, Ph.Ds, and practioners of Traditional Chinese Medicine (TCM), having worked in medical clinics and hospitals—in addition to their martial prowess, utilize healing methods quite differently from your typical allopathic doctor. Over the decades, they have collectively helped hundreds of thousands of individuals with myriad medical issues. Their sought-after medical skills, Qigong, and Internal Martial Arts are a boon to clients or practitioners.

TABLE OF CONTENTS

Acknowledgements v

Foreword xiii

Chapter 1 Making Sense of It All......................................1
Fast living, smoking habits, alcohol consumption, illicit drug use, the intake of nutrient-depleted, fat-laden food, and the now popular, caffeine-injected—energy?—drinks are causing a downward spiral into the morass of destructive moral and social behavior.

Chapter 2 Super Charge Your Body with Power Standing..10
With his Dynamic Application of Internal Awareness™ **(DAIA),** Coach Melvin helps complete novices understand internal stress release by helping you to access your inner core, tapping into an area that can positively affect your overall well-being, prevent stress from taking hold, and give you perpetual mental-physical rejuvenation.

Chapter 3 Remedy Finger & Arm Numbness................21
Heaven's Palms, a movement that shares the same principles as Power Standing, is an excellent therapy for numbness of the hands and fingers suffered by office workers, secretaries, administrative assistants, and other individuals engaged in a great deal of typing, computer keyboarding, and other repetitive tasks.

Chapter 4 Relax Like Wet Noodles 28
A relaxed movement that fully energizes the internal organs between the chest and waist as it loosens the joints of the shoulders, elbows, hands and hips.

Chapter 5 Globe Circles For Strong, Supple Neck Muscles..30
Globe Circles helps to strengthen your neck muscles while also contributing to your neck's flexibility. Prevention of repetitive motion injuries is another benefit of this exercise.

Chapter 6 Develop Centrifugal Force with Center Circles 32
The rotational effect of Center Circles on the muscle groups in the waist stimulates, develops, and empowers the function of the nerves, thereby improving mobility, flexibility and coordination. This is one of the main reasons why Tai Chi, places such importance on waist training.

Chapter 7 Put Your Hips in Orbit 34
Centrifugal Force is further developed here. This exercise extends Center Circles, helping to encourage a type of spiraling energy.

Chapter 8 *Rotate Knees* 36
These hinges are not load-bearing. They are built for load transference. These marvelous units are designed to allow the energy of body weight to bypass the knees and go straight through the legs to the feet.

Chapter 9 The Relaxing Way of Hill Climbing 37
There is no impact and very low exertion in this step that simulates climbing a steep hill, and gives your legs a good stretch.

Chapter 10 Leanin' on the Scene 38
Get a good inside leg stretch.

Chapter 11 Increase Your Stretch-A-Bility 39
For the final step you get to sit, breathe, stretch, and relax.

Chapter 12 Qigong's Relationship to Tai Chi 41
Taijiquan—mispronounced in the West as Tai Chi Chuan, and also shortened to Tai Chi—is actually an innovative Chinese martial art said to have been created by the Chen Family. However, Qigong meditation and Tai Chi are both based on theoretical principles that are inherent to Traditional Chinese Medicine (**TCM**).

Chapter 13 Your Daily Bank of Health 46
To ensure that you have enough time to condition your body's neural pathways to establish a new habit which then becomes automatic, Dr. Carl Totton favors the 100 Day Method where you commit yourself to practice a given sequence of activities every day for one hundred days. Similar to putting money in a bank which gathers interest every single day, your ROI is exceptional health.

Chapter 14 Yixingong - Standing Like a Tree For Strength, Health and Longevity..56
Dr. Painter holds a Ph.D. in Chinese Naturopathic medicine, and was the Founder/publisher of Internal Arts Magazine from 1986 - 1993, a publication devoted to scientific research of Qigong and other Asian mind-body medical principles. In his chapter, he encapsulates some of that knowledge and lets you know that committed practice of Li family Yixingong (Standing Meditation) methods produce profound results at a neurological level.

Chapter 15 Nutrition - A Trilogy of Nourishment 73
You will discover here exceptional information that, though readily available, is unfortunately the "underdog" overshadowed by repeated bombardment of multibillion dollar media marketing campaigns of junk food and pharmaceuticals. A wealth of highly nutritional, lesser-known, powerful healing foods are within this chapter and the following two chapters.

Chapter 16 Mushrooms: Some of the Most Potent, Natural Medicines on the Planet 139
Little-known by most, this "strange" plant is an unbelievable lifesaver. Some grow in various places from the earth, others grow on dead or fallen trees. But one in particular grows on living trees, escapes detection as a mushroom, yet provides near miraculous healing to your body.

Chapter 17 Three Super Food Substances 158
What do these three food substances have in common? Two of them are minerals, and the other is actually a tree. Thousands of people worldwide have benefitted from these powerful organic substances. This chapter gives a detailed, exploratory view of three of some of the most powerful substances in the world.

Conclusion 186

About the Author 188
As an innovator, the author wants you to have exceptional health and well-being, which is why he conducts extensive research on both internal and external health in order to present to you information you would not normally know about.

Special Inclusion... 196
List of Preeminent Qigong / Tai Chi Chuan Masters

FOREWORD

This is a very unique book on defeating inner stress, the deadly enemy to maximum health, happiness and peace. I like it! Coach Melvin has provided a fabulous resource that can make you victorious over all inner stress and do it superfast! With this book you will be able to release yourself from that inner stress which wreaks havoc on your body, your soul, your relationships...and your life. He gives simple, easy to understand advice that is unique and powerful!

This book is full of amazing, innovative insights and brilliant wisdom on how to eliminate inner stress that impacts people in all areas of life including business, parenting, jobs...basically life in general. As a savvy trainer and an expert in leadership, Coach Melvin brings a wealth of experience, tools, stories and strategies to ensure that you get, and stay stress-free, in your heart and in your mind and soul.

With this book you will be able to "throw out the trash" that has been causing stress, then replace it with pristine principles and methods that work. What he teaches will rejuvenate you daily, weekly and forever.

As an internationally recognized success expert I can say that the Coach has done a great job in explaining how to make "peace" in any area of life a reality. Read it NOW!

Jack M. Zufelt
"Mentor to Millions"
International Speaker & Author of the
#1 best-selling book, The DNA of Success....Now in 15 languages

Seen and heard on 2,000 radio and TV talk shows including **The TODAY SHOW and PBS**

www.TheDNAofSuccessSystem.com
www.JackZufeltSpeaks.com

Chapter 1 - Making Sense of It All

Thanks to split-second takes, and subliminal messages or images in television commercials, people are obsessed with non-stop action made popular by the entertainment industry. The speed and action of adrenalin-pumping basketball, the hustle and power displayed in football, the barbarism shown in the clinch fighting, throws and takedowns, joint locks, pins and other grappling holds demonstrated by contestants in WrestleMania, and now the newly-regulated popularity of mixed martial arts (MMA), bring the thrill of victory or the agony of defeat. Throw into the mix squeals of excitement from exhilarating theme park rides, and the roar of the crowd as the peals of high-speed cars thunder around the track from The Indy 500. Top all of that off with attention to the latest fad, and you have capricious individuals, or what is termed in Chinese as, a person with a "monkey mind."

It is a given that the exploits of this fast-paced nation are compounded by many stress-induced physical disorders. Assisting this, but causing a downward spiral into the morass of destructive moral and social behavior, are: the smoking habits, alcohol consumption, illegal drug use, the intake of nutrient-depleted, fat-laden food, and the now popular caffeine-injected—energy?—drinks. Yet, to seemingly have the answer for practically anything that ails anyone, our ever-present friend, the pharmaceutical industry, takes full advantage of this by mass marketing both prescription and practically useless over-the-counter drugs of every sort through the myriad distribution channels of physician offices, and via the thousands of nationwide drug store and supermarket chains. People just do not take enough time and are not consistent enough with daily fluid (H_2O) intake, exercise, and meditation to reflect on the stillness and truly know themselves. Instead, they rely on pills to control stress, pills to calm anxiety and yet more pills to help them sleep after the stimulants of their busy lifestyle have made them uptight insomniacs.

One of the biggest problems with people is the stamina-reducing habit of incorrect breathing patterns—especially the lifting of the chest when asked to take a deep breath. Actually, lifting the chest high and trying to force oxygen into the body constricts the tissues around the rib cage causing you to bring in only a small amount of air, just barely enough to maintain the body's basic functions. Breath is a vital, powerful tool. When you develop awareness of your particular breathing pattern, you can adapt it to accommodate sports, change your emotions, increase or decrease muscular tension, activate your organs, strengthen your singing or speaking voice, and even to support or change the curvature of your spine. And you thought breath just oxygenated your blood!

By working with the flow of breath in your body, you basically go beneath all the harmful and damaging movement patterns you've learned throughout your life and reset your body in a neutral place. This is, of course, a process and takes practice and patience

So What Is The Book on Internal STRESS Release: Get Powerful Health and Nutritional Secrets about?

Basically, this book empowers you with the knowledge you need to make informed, and better choices regarding the integrity of your health. And, by practicing and involving yourself in the program offered by world-renown naturophathic doctor, Dr. John P. Painter, or the 100-day method offered by Board-Certified psychologist, Dr. Carl Totton, you will have much better health and live a more stress-free life in this ad-driven, commercialized, chaotic world. Coach Melvin's Dynamic Application of Internal Awareness™(DAIA) program will help you to understand internal energy cultivation in detail. This is referred to by the Chinese as chi, and represented by the Chinese character 气, which can mean gas, air, or breath. You will learn that, when you breathe with relaxed, focused, conscious thought, this can effectively impact a peculiar type of energy produced within the body. You can, thus, manipulate it just as easily as one controls the movement of the fingers, arms, head, and eyes, with conscious or subconscious thought.

In essence, the main focus of the book is to empower you to use your mind, in unison with the produced energy, to deter the emotional aftermath from the tsunami of negative stress. By having this ability, you can actually dissolve pent up, negative stress energy and release it from your body like opening a soda releases the built up gas within the container. This release prevents you from acting impulsively and irrationally. Let's take a real-life scenario. You are out in public when you experience a strong need to use the restroom. You hurry in an attempt to find one. As the pressure within you builds, you suddenly become aware of your bladder. Not having found a restroom, you become more frantic. The bladder pressure increases unbearably. When the pressure of the bladder reaches the critical stage you will shuffle, jump, scream, run, knocking anybody out of the way, and practically make a fool of yourself attempting to get to the restroom to relieve—release that pressure—yourself. Thus, the book's title: The Book on Internal STRESS Release. By incorporating what's offered here into your daily schedule and judiciously following it, you can expect the following important benefits:

Enhanced health and stamina.

Reduced emotional and mental stress.

Intense inner-power and mental clarity.

There is a plethora of information on chi. It is available everywhere, especially via the Internet, from a wide variety of sources both well-informed, and misinformed. These misinformed sources are causing the misperception of the word chi. That word chi has been wrongly translated here in America, becoming generalized to be synonymous with energy. Nothing can be farther from the truth.

One of the many reasons people are so confused about the issue of chi is because of the total difference in culture, language, and religion between the East and the West. Attempts to translate with limited command of the English language resulted in the current colloquial—and inaccurate—term chi to mean energy. Many teachers use abstracts such as: heart-center, heart-mind, third eye center, and **The Gate of Life,** to talk about or explain certain points. Others (many of whom cannot speak the Chinese language, but use Chinese words, names, or phrases they have picked up) use these abstracts and much of the traditional symbolism on non-Chinese-speaking students in an attempt to impress them with their ability to verbalize those words. As any translator will tell you, any time that thoughts, symbols, images, and cultural idioms are translated from one language to another, there is always some loss of meaning. Cultural metaphors do not translate easily. The "mind map" changes, no matter how hard one tries to maintain it.

I am not attempting to make light of the fact that teachers of Qigong have no relevant qualifications to teach effectively. However, if I am studying under a highly-qualified, American martial arts master, I would rather he communicate with me in the plain, everyday English language we both have an excellent command of than for him to try to enthrall me with his vain attempts at Oriental phraseology and unnecessary abstracts and symbolism to muddle up my learning experience.

Chi is just one of, and the first component, used to produce energy. That process needs two additional components which form a trio of elements joining forces for the production of this so-called mystical energy that the uninitiated call chi. Water and nutritious foods that we should consume are the other two components that are absolutely essential. Those three: air (chi), water, and food, are the vital elements that work in unison to produce energy. This intimacy exploits the natural synergy between the elements. Within the body, this synergistic phenomenon is ubiquitous. The quality of the energy depends solely on the quality of each of these three elements. The elements are listed in the order of relative importance. Notice the order: air, then water, then food. Of the three, air is superior and of utmost importance. You can survive for mere minutes without it. Generally speaking, there is a popular term called: "The Rule of Threes." This rule states that one can survive only three minutes without oxygen, three days without water, and three weeks without food. Of course, there are always exceptions to rules, but in this case, the exception may potentially cause irreparable damage to the brain if it goes too long without oxygen. Since the human body is approximately 65 to 75 percent fluid, extreme harm will befall humans if no water is ingested over a lengthy period. Lastly, since the body extracts necessary vitamins from food sources. Energy production will continue at a downward spiral until the body expires from the lack of this component. It will continue to supply the source from stored body nutrients which it extracts its vitamins and minerals until the source is completed.

As popular misconception makes mention to this chi misnomer, so as not to confuse you, the reader of this book, let's be clear on the term "energy." The mind is not able to create energy. It can manage and direct the flow of energy only after the body produces it. In essence, every human and animal on the face of the planet breathes, drinks, and eats. Therefore, their bodies produce energy whether they think about it or not. A basic comparison could be your job and direct deposit. You work to produce income. Over a period of time, that income is automatically deposited (stored) in your bank account. Now, the money is there whether you make use of it or not. The same is true for energy. Your body works to produce it. Over a period of time (minutes, hours), depending on the type of food you consume, that energy is deposited (stored) in the "bank account" of your body. Now, the energy is there whether you make use of it or not. This energy does not build up, however. It actually dissipates as the body uses it and continues to produce more—perpetual ebb (dissipation) and flow (production).

Both physics and physiology play a role in cell respiration, so leaders and students in those disciplines will be concerned about the formula of this process that takes place inside the body cells where oxygen reacts with glucose to yield carbon dioxide, water, heat and energy (ATP). ATP is Adenosine Triphosphate. Aerobic cellular respiration actually has four stages. Each is important. Each stage could not happen without the one preceding it. The simplified formula for aerobic cellular respiration is:

$$C_6H_{12}O_6 + 6O_2 \rightarrow 6CO_2 + 6H_2O + \text{Energy (as ATP)}$$
(Glucose (sugar) + Oxygen → Carbon dioxide + Water + Energy (as ATP))[1]

ATP is this energy that is wrongly translated as chi. This is the energy that is generated by the oxygen from our air intake. It is not an energy floating freely around in space to be absorbed by someone. In essence chi is the air we breathe in space to provide oxygen to our body cells to generate energy by the Cellular Respiration chemical process. Chi Kung is a method that involves breathing exercise with or without muscle movements for peace of mind and the health of the body.

That leads us to the validity of this book. The Book on Internal STRESS Release: Get Powerful Health and Nutritional Secrets, aims to help guide you into withdrawing some of this energy from your body bank account and using it for effective purposes. Just like you go to the bank to withdraw a certain amount of money and go to different places to apply (spend) it, so it is with energy. You use your mind to withdraw a certain amount of energy and, with that awareness, you go to different internal parts of your body to apply

[1] Source, Simple English Wikipedia, http://simple.wikipedia.org/wiki/Cellular_respiration

(spend) it.

Though qigong comprises breathing, physical, and mental training methods based on Chinese philosophy, actually engaging in its practice instead of merely obtaining intellectual knowledge about it goes far in helping you to understand and actually apply it. While application of it may vary between schools, most qigong forms are categorized into four types of training: dynamic, stationary, meditative, and Traditional Chinese Medicine (TCM).

- **Dynamic**

    This type of training involves relaxed, flowing, choreographed movement that is coordinated with breath and awareness. Examples include the slow stylized movements similar to that of the Yang or Wu styles of Tai Chi

- **Stationary**

    This type of training involves holding postures for sustained periods of time. For example, in one system of Chinese martial art called Yi-Quan, static stance training is emphasized. In the healing form "Eight Pieces of Brocade" a different system, training is based on a series of static postures.

- **Meditative**

    Basically, this type of training utilizes breath awareness. It focuses on metaphysical concepts such as chi circulation. In Taoist and traditional Chinese medicinal practice, the meditative focus is on cultivating chi in your body's energy center (about an inch below the navel) and balancing chi flow in meridians and other pathways.

- **Traditional Chinese Medicine (TCM)**

    Many systems of qigong training include the use of external agents such as ingestion of herbs, massage, physical manipulation, or application of various types of elixirs. For example, specialized food and drinks are used in some medical and Taoist forms, whereas massage and body manipulation are sometimes used in martial arts forms. In some medical systems, a qigong master uses non-contact treatment, purportedly guiding qi through his or her own body into the body of another person.

- **Taking Responsibility**

    Stress comes from anxiety, which is your worrying over the unforeseen outcome of an event either real or imagined. However, most people choose to focus on a negative outcome; they become tense, and stress sets in. Nevertheless, until you accept responsibility for the role you play in creating or maintaining it, your stress level will remain outside your control. There is subtleness to how your own stress-inducing thoughts, feelings, and behaviors overtake your mind. You may know that you're constantly worried about work deadlines, for example. But, maybe it's your procrastination, rather than the actual demands of your job, that contributes to this deadline stress.

To identify your true sources of stress, look closely at your habits, attitude, and excuses:

- Do you explain away stress as temporary, "I just have a million things going on right now." even though you can't remember the last time you took a breather?

- Do you define stress as an integral part of your work or home life, "Things are always crazy around here." or as a part of your personality, "I have a lot of nervous energy, that's all."?

- Do you blame your stress on other people or outside events, or view it as entirely normal and unexceptional?

If you find that any or all of these are true to you, and are willing to admit it, then you are more than halfway to resolving this important health-threatening issue. The next chapter will provide certain benefits to you if you commit yourself to consistent practice. If you are extremely pressed for time and can spare only ten minutes, then invest that time in Standing Meditation, as the secret to success is consistency; it should be performed daily. The other exercises may be done three to four times a week.

To be brutally honest, if you expect to obtain excellent benefits, Standing Meditation should become a way of life as opposed to just *something you do*. Just as you have a certain routine you do practically every day without fail, such as waking up, going to the bathroom to rinse or wash your face, starting your morning coffee, picking out what you're going to wear for the day, taking a quick shower, constantly checking the time, rushing to do this or that—you should also *make* time for Standing Meditation.

By making these steps a routine, you will get better at it and begin carving out more minutes for it. Then, you will begin to notice that it has a domino effect on the whole day. Your day will go easier than had you not practiced these life-changing steps. The principles of meditation will begin to manifest themselves to you like an open book. You will begin practicing them even when you are not in the formal practice postures. For when you stop, your level of attainment begins to deteriorate. Continuous practice of it is required to maintain this effect.

Chapter 2 - Super Charge Your Body with Power Standing

Dynamic Application of Internal Awareness™(DAIA)

Meditation started becoming a trendy lifestyle choice and a source of a lot of conversation as far back as the sixties for baby boomers when there was a big interest in eastern religions and things that were exotic and new. But, while many of the flash-in-the-pan interests in exotic religions during that time-frame faded from the life style of baby boomers, meditation has endured and is now common practice. It is a resource that has benefited this generation in every decade of their lives.

There is good reason meditation has endured and even grown in popularity far beyond any religious context. Meditation has tremendous benefits for virtually every aspect of life. Those who integrate it into their daily lifestyles can experience those benefits virtually as soon as they start. You don't have to be a guru at meditation to realize benefits from the very first time you give it a try. Some of those benefits include:

- **Calming**. Because the act of meditation calls for you to bring your thoughts into captivity and to still your mind and focus it, that sense of your soul being in turmoil eases and you are able to address the cause of your anxiety and see a solution more clearly because your emotions are not clouding the issue.
- **Focus and concentration**. The great thing about meditation is that the effects of meditation continue past those few moments when you are meditating. Those few moments of calm create an atmosphere of focus and clarity of thought that goes on throughout your day, helping you focus your mind and more easily concentrate when you need to.
- **Reduction of stress and mental anxiety**. So often the stress that comes out of problems and difficulties is dominated by emotional reactions even more than by the problem itself. Meditation clears away

the effects of the stress, making it easier for you to solve the problem itself.
- **Reduction of physical anxiety**. The process of meditation involves extended periods of quiet, deep breathing. This simple action floods the brain with oxygen and energizes blood flow throughout the body. This, in turn, refreshes tired muscles and causes your entire physical system to relax and release pent-up anxiety.
- **Improved sleep and digestion**. The refreshed oxygen-rich blood flow that comes from the session of meditation, takes action immediately on the digestive system often reducing or eliminating digestive problems and even easing the symptoms of ulcers. Because the mind is relaxed and well supplied with vital oxygen and blood flow, sleep comes more easily and is more recuperative.

Coach Melvin puts emphasis on the DAIA Method how you are able to get powerful health benefits, release tension—which is the benefactor of stress—and greatly enhance your physical and energetic body. This practice is easy to integrate into your lifestyle, and you can go at your own pace, learning to become better at meditation and grow in your ability to use it.

Power Standing using t*he DAIA Method* is actually a type of meditation. It is profoundly easy to do. The classic image of a practitioner in "lotus position" going into a virtual trance and sometimes reciting sounds such as, "Ohmmmmmm" and other sounds is the extreme of the discipline. However, the DAIA method we use is a radically different adaptation. Any of us can profit greatly from the health benefits it brings without going to the extremes. The validity of DAIA is so that the student learns how to relax and connect the body structure internally. For example: gently tucking in your tail bone pulls down the shoulders. Standing in a balanced, natural position gives a novice the opportunity to focus and work on being aware of what is going on inside the body without the added confusion of having to move simultaneously.

Heaven's Palms adds a very controlled measure of movement so that the body awareness built up in DAIA may be taken to a more challenging, but not overwhelming, situation. Becoming proficient in

Heaven's Palms actually trains particular Tai Chi principles in a limited setting. This gives the novice an awareness of those principles that can be translated at a later stage of development into the more complicated complete Tai Chi routine. However, beginning DAIA will launch you on to your journey of experiencing Tai Chi's benefits from the very first session. Small wonder the author, who coined the term, *Dynamic Application of Internal Awareness*™ *(DAIA)*, has continued, through the decades, to be an enthusiastic proponent of Power Standing meditation. Practically anyone—not just baby boomers—may enjoy the tremendous benefits offered within the pages of this book.

In 1994, because Western scientists, using high tech equipment, discovered the Chinese meridian system, the American Medical Association (AMA) approved acupuncture as a legitimate therapy. Interestingly enough, if you were to ask an Oriental Medical Doctor *how* acupuncture works, he would probably have a good laugh. We Americans always want to know how something works. To the Chinese, the simple fact that it works is enough. As to its "how," they have little interest. In fact, I don't think anyone can tell you how acupuncture works. They can tell you only how to work it!

Here, in the West, we seem to feel that disease begins with symptoms. Physicians will tell you that the disease process begins much earlier, at a cellular level. This is only logical. To the Chinese, disease begins with a disruption in energy flow (qi) through the meridian system. **Qigong is designed to make that energy flow return to normal.**

Power Standing - *Dynamic Application of Internal Awareness*™ **(DAIA)**

As a warmup, DAIA is of premier importance. It is based on a widely practiced *internal* exercise within the Chinese Qigong (Chi Gung) system. Although there are other names for it, the important thing to know is that, through diligent practice, you will obtain a type of awareness second to none, and of a type of power that will be accessible to you both consciously and subconsciously. You will actualize the powerful energy being manifested within your body and you will have the ability to command it at will. It is unfortunate that, though many marvel at the profound nature of this exercise, become interested in it, and pursue it, few are committed enough to make the time and effort to realize the true benefits of this powerful energy that resides within.

For the few who diligently pursue DAIA, making it a life style, this newfound sense of internal body awareness, you will find, will meld with other aspects of your life in a positive way. Things that you have normally taken for granted or have performed with some effort will be done with very minimal exertion or expended energy. These activities might include: making a dash for a bus, walking up a hill or many flights of stairs, carrying heavy loads, stooping, cooking, doing laundry, and just about every other sort of daily movement. Because the basic requirement of this exercise is simply "standing," you will develop the ability to stand for long periods of time, if your job requires it, without any adverse effects on your body. For example, without going deep into the annals of DAIA, just take the very basics of it: physically relaxing, tucking your tail bone, and slightly sinking your weight (where your knees bend a little). This alone will absorb some of the burden of your body's own weight as well as any added weight or outside pressure. At times, my four-year-old daughter, Velvet, gets tired and sleepy when we're out and about. So, I have to pick her up and carry her. That may not seem like much of a load, but when you've been walking around a huge mall for several hours window shopping or purchasing a few things, carrying a backpack full of... well you know the stuff you have to carry when you have small kids, it can take a toll on your body. But by utilizing this DAIA method: breathing, relaxing, tucking and sinking, the burden is significantly lifted.

Begin DAIA by standing upright (not erect with locked knees), being relaxed, looking straight ahead, arms hanging loosely at your sides, and your feet together. Do not lift your chest or suck in the abdomen like you see soldiers doing while standing at attention in a military formation. Simply allow your chest and abdomen to relax.

Next, bend the knees very slightly while opening the legs (left foot steps toward the left), with the feet a comfortable distance (approximately shoulder-width) apart and your weight evenly distributed on both feet. After stepping into this position do not lean or bend forward at the waist. The feeling you should have is a little buoyancy. The weight of the body goes straight down through the thighs (with the knees acting as the hinges) and through the legs to the center of the feet. (See illustration.) Turn your palms rearward and gently tuck your hips under. Close your eyes and lift the tip of your tongue to the roof of your mouth (palate), where you will keep it throughout the duration of DAIA. Your tongue position is as though you are about to say "leave." While you are in this position, breathe as an infant does. No infant in the world has a big chest and tight abdominal muscles. Look at the body of an infant while he or she is breathing. From the moment of birth—all things being equal—infants begin with proper breathing patterns.

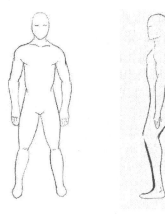

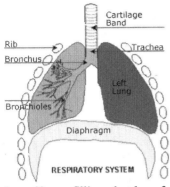

The nose, trachea, lungs, and diaphragm are part of the body's respiratory system. Keeping in mind how a baby breathes, do likewise. Using your imagination, feel the air sinking down (traveling on a path) to an area a couple of inches below your navel. Once again, do not lift the chest as you breathe. You are not actually breathing *into* the belly. You are, in effect, filling both of your lungs entirely with oxygen. Done correctly, the downward pressure on your diaphragm[2] causes it to contract. With this increased downward pressure on the diaphragm, your abdomen expands, and contracts with the lessened pressure when the lungs are being emptied. In essence, the diaphragm falls and rises, beginning at some point in time after conception until your last breath, in a perpetual, down-up cycle, in unison with your breathing. As stated previously, this movement is tantamount to the rise and fall of a sleeping infant's belly.

With your eyes and mouth closed, and your tongue pressing against your palate there are five major areas we will emphasize.

5-Point Emphasis

- Breathing

- Shoulders

- Lower back muscles

- Hips

- Toes

---

[2] The diaphragm, which performs an important function in respiration, is a sheet of internal skeletal muscle (see diagram) that extends across the bottom of the rib cage, separating the ribs, lungs and heart above from the abdominal area below.

As you observe the 5-Point Emphasis as shown above, realize breathing is the first, and most important, of the 5-Point Emphasis. Your eyes are closed, hands loosely at your sides and weight centered, gently tuck in your hips while continuing to breathe in slowly and deeply (not forcefully) and expelling all of the "bad" air. Now, beginning with the crown of your head—put your awareness there— let go of those tense scalp muscles. Just relax. At this area, start scanning downward centimeter by centimeter, inch by inch. Let your awareness slowly flow across the top of your scalp and continue downward on all sides as your body relaxes each part. You relax in this gradual way, as water falls on your body in the shower. When you stand directly under the shower head, the water first lands on the top of your head. It flows down on all sides of your body while pushing the sweat, dirt, and shed skin downward to your feet, and ultimately into the drain. This is an example of what your mind— your awareness—does as you relax. Think of all the mental stress, which leads to physical tension, slowly draining downward from the top of your head until it reaches your feet, and then flows down into the ground. At advanced stages of training, one can direct negative stress energy into the ground as well as pull up beneficial energy from the ground.

At this point in learning to breathe, take your time and go very slowly as you release any strength or tension in your head, eyes, temples, mouth, and jaw. It is imperative that you do not rush through this. Rushing will not get you to where you want to go. Continue downward to the neck, shoulders, chest, upper back, arms, hands, and fingers. Relax all of the mid-abdominal area, the lower abdominal area, waist, hips, buttocks, thighs, knees, legs, ankles, and finally your feet. When done properly (with months of practice), this process should take a *minimum* of fifteen minutes. Once again, with your mind (awareness), think of the sensation of water flowing down your body in slow motion. Afterward, you should notice an overall difference in your entire body. The inside feels invigorated while the outside feels totally relaxed. If you do this exercise on a daily basis (or at least several days within a week), you will notice immediate results in the release of tension. Furthermore, you will continue to experience daily rejuvenation throughout your body. To produce perpetual benefits and to enable a person to heal various symptoms of illness, however, this practice must become a lifestyle change. For example, as long as you continue living you must breathe, drink and eat. Stopping either, for any significant amount of time, you will expire. Likewise, if you stop this practice of conscious relaxation, you will not experience its exceptional health benefits.

It's only fair to warn you that you will experience "strange" sensations subsequent to commencing the practice of DAIA. After the first five or more minutes—if you hold it that long or longer, you may feel your body becoming very warm or experience a tingling sensation. You may have a sensation of coldness or your legs may begin to vibrate or shake uncontrollably. You may perspire very heavily; some people feel the sensation of beads of sweat rolling down their back, practically driving them crazy. You also may find that, as you relax one particular area and move on to the next to begin relaxing it, the area you previously relaxed has subtly tensed again. These are normal manifestations as your mind becomes increasingly aware of what the energy is doing within your body. Like an infant expressing herself by flailing the arms and legs around without thoughtful control, your body expresses your attempt to become aware of energy by the above manifestations. These strange feelings will come to an end as your awareness of the energy within your body increases.

Upon completion of Power Standing, *slowly* open your eyes. Do not open them quickly, as the energy of the light entering them will shock your system. While your eyes are gradually opening, look downward through your eyelashes for several seconds. Continue slowly opening your eyelids, and gently look straight ahead. Take mental inventory of your whole body for a few seconds. Consider how refreshed your entire body feels.

Performing DAIA consistently will go far in keeping you clear-headed and giving you the ability to respond to stressful situations without hesitation. This natural-posture relaxation exercise is beginning to be practiced by more and more people besides those who practice the martial arts. The exercise has been known to keep stress under control for some corporate executives responsible for major decisions affecting the growth of Fortune 500 companies. Some allopathic doctors (MD)'s are even using this exercise themselves to relieve the stress of treating multiple patients every day, or standing for hours in surgery. As well, they are suggesting it to their patients before or instead of dispensing prescription medication.

For a general sense of relaxation, I suggest performing DAIA for five minutes daily. Actually, until this is mastered, the body spends the first five minutes physically relaxing. However, over a period of weeks, gradually increase the time from five to fifteen minutes to help keep the results of negative stress at bay. For people who want to attain a high degree of mental acuteness, relaxation, balance, and control of the seemingly intangible chi-manifested energy within the body, daily practice of between fifteen to thirty minutes is normally sufficient. If you have ample time and want to have a better understanding of the ability to access the full spectrum of your internal body energy kinesthetically, I suggest that you attend one of the many seminars taught around the country by bona fide Qigong teachers. You can also obtain *Opening the Energy Gates of Your Body: Chi Gung for Lifelong Health* by Bruce Frantzis, an internationally known master of the Chinese fighting and healing arts. He teaches a complete and varied system of these arts, going into great detail regarding the study of internal energy of the body. For more information and to purchase his book, visit his Web site at www.energyarts.com.

Ideally, you will enjoy greater health benefits by making DAIA a part of your daily routine. This exercise involves no physical movement other than slow, deep, rhythmic breathing where your diaphragm falls and rises. Only the mind is dynamically involved to sense the inner workings of your body as you stand still, completely relaxed in a natural posture. While you may enjoy good health benefits from this practice at home, feel you are following instructions properly, and your movements appear to be correct, I suggest that you seek a qualified Qigong/Tai Chi instructor to check your progress. The practice of this exercise under the guidance of a qualified instructor may result in your having the ability to perform the nuances in movement. For example, "tuck in your tailbone" is not something that everyone can understand. A qualified instructor can better assist you with that. All of the masters listed in this publication are highly qualified to assist you. However, if those listed here are not in or near where you reside, please visit QigongInstitute.org, a worldwide listing, for a school near you.

Throughout DAIA, remember to keep the tip of your tongue in constant contact with your palate. This is one of the major channels of the body through which energy flows. The tongue could be thought of as a light switch. With your tongue contacting your palate, your energy flows smoothly. All Chinese internal martial arts emphasize, during the training process, some form of DAIA. In some systems, it is the first concept studied and the first skill a person must acquire before proceeding to learn moving exercises. Some Chinese masters will not instruct a student further until that student has practiced DAIA concepts for at least one year. Especially to those who are not familiar with the internal martial arts, this requirement may seem strange and difficult to understand. Yet the standing practice is justified by the sense of relaxed, connected strength that it imparts. This state of tranquility can then be carried into movement. By spending enough time on what you might consider to be a rather boring exercise, you will discover that the body has become both healthier and better conditioned. The complex muscle movements needed for the application of the techniques illustrated in this book will become a habit if DAIA is first mastered. That is why Coach Melvin is so adamant in emphasizing this practice before proceeding.

Knowing DAIA well is the difference between having the ability to dissolve stress or allowing it to unnerve you. To develop the ability to instantaneously dissolve practically any type of mental stress, you must spend the requisite amount of time building your foundation. Attempting to absorb everything too quickly and then having scant results would be disheartening to say the least. This exercise may seem simple, perhaps too simple to be effective. Bear in mind, however, that in this situation the simplest item from an outward point of view can be very complex. A good example is the garden flower. Look at how a flower grows in the soil, basking in the rays of the sun, taking in the oxygen, and swaying in the gentle breeze. Yet, a hubbub of energetic activity is taking place within the flower. Understand that concept, and you will understand the first step of DAIA. Thoroughly understanding and practicing it will lead to a better understanding and achievement of the next two exercises: Heaven's Palms and Wet Noodles.

As you proceed to Heaven's Palms, it is imperative to maintain the state of relaxation you attained, as you will commence slow, deliberate, waist turns and relaxed, smooth, arm circles and spirals.

Chapter 3 - Remedy Finger & Arm Numbness

Heaven's Palms is an excellent remedy for numbness of the hands and fingers suffered by typists, data processors, secretaries, administrative assistants, and other individuals engaged in a lot of computer keyboarding. Releasing stress begins with having a strong desire to take charge of your thoughts, emotions, schedule, and the way you deal with problems. The bills won't stop coming and your career and family responsibilities will always be demanding. Unfortunately, too many people in society—I believe as a result of commercialism—use popular but extremely unhealthy ways of coping with stress. These symptomatic coping strategies may temporarily conceal stress, but they cause more damage in the long run. These coping strategies might include:

- Smoking
- Drinking (alcohol)
- Overeating or under eating
- Zoning out for hours in front of the TV or computer
- Withdrawing from friends, family, and activities
- Using pharmaceuticals to relax
- Sleeping too much
- Procrastinating
- Filling up every minute of the day to avoid facing problems
- Taking out your stress on others (lashing out, angry outbursts, physical violence)

Fortunately, sufficient time (meaning several weeks) spent practicing DAIA—Power Standing, is enough to crush your desire to participate in most of the above vices. However, length of participation in bad habits, like the inhalation of nicotine-laden tobacco, poisons your vital internal components throughout your body, interferes with your respiratory system, and causes a chemical imbalance within. This imbalance wreaks havoc on your emotions, producing unbearable cravings for more and stronger doses of the substance. Many who smoke also participate in the drinking of alcoholic beverages. Alcoholic substances slowly destroy brain cells, (which, by the way, are not regenerated) causing diminished mental acuity and may, over time, contribute to dementia. Further damaging the synergistic integrity of the body's internal components is the ingestion of prescription, and OTC medication, tranquilizers, mood elevators, and various types of social or recreational drugs. In many cases, these are mixed with regular smoking of cigarettes and imbibing of alcoholic beverages. All of these types of poisonous substances individually or together work against the body.

Eloquent, multi-billion dollar production of young, smiling, Hollywood models in picturesque settings, advertising the "goodness" of those substances actually tricks the mind into believing all of this is euphoric. Why settle for unpleasant or health-threatening side effects from mind-altering drugs? Most notably this habit takes its toll on your outward appearance and functions of your body and mind. These vices manifest themselves in such things as: withdrawn, hollow-eyed, hazy-eyed, sleepy-looking, unkempt, loss of lean weight, forgetfulness, mood-swings, inability to control bowel movement, slurred speech, constant guttural coughing, shortness of breath, anger, the feeling that somebody's watching you, suppressed feelings, hyper-arousal that results in being easily startled, and flashbacks.

Adding Heaven's Palms is like adding a bridge that connects you to "the other side," and further reinforces your determination to quell these powerful, negative forces attempting to supplant your struggle. It is a solution that will not take much time. Time is your most precious commodity. Emotions can affect your physical health just as much as your mental mindset. Completing Heaven's Palms establishes discipline to help balance the mind and the body. There is no separation between mind and body. What you feel mentally can, and often does, have a direct impact on your physical health.

Again, after completing Power Standing, your goal is to remain in the tranquility it produces while proceeding to Heaven's Palms, which introduces smooth, gentle movement. This important step involves movement of the whole body, gently shifting from side to side with emphasis on turning at the waist. Brought into this gentle, shifting, turning movement is the totally relaxed state of mind that became apparent after you completed Power Standing (Standing Meditation).

In essence, through these gentle movements you actually obtain all the benefits a normal Tai Chi routine would provide you, without having to learn all of the complicated movements.

Regarding Tai Chi, I salute Dr. Daniel Richman a board-certified anesthesiologist who has specialized in Pain Management since 1991. His specialty is Anesthesiology and Musculoskeletal & Interventional Pain Management. His subspecialty is Pain Medicine and Acupuncture. Additionally, his special expertise is in orthopedic-related chronic pain, low back pain and neuropathic pain. Dr. Richman received an award as one of the top doctors in pain management in the New York area. He has acquired extensive medical knowledge, and access to some of the most advanced medical equipment. Yet, this doctor, who suffered excruciating pain stemming from wind surfing, has spent eight years practicing Tai Chi Chuan which relieved his pain. Thus, with all his training in the most advanced technology in medicine, he is recommending people including his patients to take the ancient Chinese martial art/ healing art Tai Chi for pain relief. Dr. Richman practices from ninety minutes to two hours several days a week.

Commence Heaven's Palms

Begin by gently shifting your weight from one leg to the other. After a few seconds of doing that, lift your arms slowly in front of your body to chest height. Do not lock the elbows. Keep them slightly bent. Let the wrists and fingers relax and go limp. As you continue to shift from side to side with your arms out in front, begin turning at the waist toward the shifting leg. Each time the weight shifts from one leg to the other, turn the body slightly in that direction.

Once you are shifting smoothly from side to side, add the arm movement by lowering one arm while the other is extended. For example, when you shift and turn to the left side, your left arm sinks down by your thigh, palm facing downward. While you are doing this, imagine that you are pushing an air-filled rubber ball down until it is under water. Your right arm extended in front of you rotates—from the fingertips to the elbow joint—toward the right until the palm faces up. The elbows do not lock but remain slightly bent. Turn at the waist to the point where there is a slight resistance of your waist turning further. Do not attempt to twist your upper body past that point, as attempting to turn too much causes twisting of the spine.

When the shifting/turning and movements to the left side have reached the maximum without strain, immediately begin shifting and turning to your right side. Your right arm extended in front of you begins rotating, again from the fingertips to the elbow joint, counterclockwise. As you continue turning to the right, let your right arm sink down by your thigh as you imagine pushing with your palm an air-filled rubber ball down until it is under water. As this arm drops, do not lock the elbow at the end of the movement.

As this arm drops, do not lock the elbow at the end of the movement. Simultaneously with your shifting and turning, your left hand and arm begin rising as it rotates counterclockwise on the elbow axis until your palm faces up. Continue this shifting from one leg to the other, turning at the waist as your hands and arms rotate smoothly, changing position in conjunction with your turning. Perform this exercise for a minimum of two minutes, three times a week. That is enough to gain significant benefits. However, to gain exceptional benefits, try to work progressively up to fifteen minutes every day. The important point to remember as you are slowly shifting and turning is to *stay relaxed*. Continue mentally monitoring all of your body parts. Be aware that the shoulders, lower back area, and thighs do not become tense but continue to stay relaxed through the entire exercise. As a reminder, the tip of your tongue maintains contact with your palate. Keep your mouth closed and lips together but relaxed. Do not clench your teeth tightly. Just breathe deeply in and out through your nose.

IMPORTANT NOTE:

The Psoas Muscle

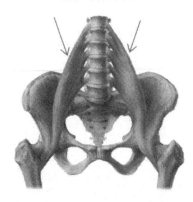

Psoas Muscle

In your rear, lower abdominal area there is a very important set of muscles called the psoas (so-as) and are the hip flexor muscles that are particularly sensitive to emotional states. They lift the thighs as you walk, and act in conjunction with the spinal muscles to support the lumbar spine. They originate on the lowest thoracic vertebra and each of the five lumbar vertebrae of the lower back, extending down through the pelvis to attach on the inside of the upper femur. They cross three major joints—the hip socket, the joint between the lumbar spine and the sacrum (L5-S1), and the sacroiliac joint (SI joint between the sacrum and the pelvis). So it's easy to see that if the psoas is not healthy and strong, there are major repercussions throughout the body.

Chronic contraction of the psoas, whether from stress or repetitive activity, limits range of movement in the hip sockets, with the frequent result of strain in the lumbar spine and the knees. When tension in the psoas is asymmetrical, that is, one side is more contracted than the other, the resulting tilt of the pelvis effectively shortens one leg relative to the other, and causes compensation up the spine into the neck as the head tries to stay level. Tension also shortens the trunk and reduces room for the viscera, so the organs don't work as efficiently. On top of that, when the pelvis, spine, and legs are misaligned, the weight of the torso is no longer carried easily through the bones, stability is compromised, and the psoas ends up trying to stabilize the pelvis rather than moving freely in its hip-flexing function. With a healthy psoas the weight is borne through the bones, and walking is initiated at the solar plexus instead of the knee or hip joint.

Through its attachments to the thoracic and lumbar vertebrae, the psoas affects a number of other important muscles, including the diaphragm, the trapezius, and the quadratus lumborum, which also attach on these vertebrae. Through these muscles, tension in the psoas has the potential to seriously compromise structural integrity and physiological functioning throughout the upper torso as well as the pelvis and abdomen. If the upper segment of the psoas is tight and constricted, the lumbar spine hyperextends, the chest collapses, the lower ribs thrust forward, and breathing patterns are affected. Many problems in stability and alignment in asanas, lower back discomfort or injury, integration between the pelvis and the chest, meditation sitting postures, and dysfunctional breathing patterns are directly related to tension in the psoas.

Many individuals, being unaware of the psoas muscle, may mistakenly believe they are experiencing kidney pain since the kidneys are in very close proximity. Most of the exercises shown in these chapters will result in your psoas muscles functioning at peak performance levels if a program such as this becomes a lifestyle.

Chapter 4 - Relax Like Wet Noodles

In Wet Noodles, keep your feet in the same position as for Heaven's Palms, and continue to be relaxed while you shift your weight from side to side, one leg to the other. However, now the shifting will speed up a little more than in Heaven's Palms. Let your arms drop by your sides and hang loosely. As you begin shifting to one side and turning at the waist, the arms will naturally swing freely.

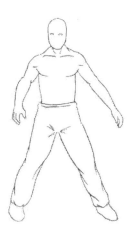

Turning at the waist in one direction will cause one arm to lightly tap the front of your body with the palm of your hand while the other arm will lightly tap the rear of your body with the back of your hand. When you shift and turn in the other direction, the arms will swing accordingly, then, your arms will tap the opposite sides of your body. Do not use your arm muscles to control and swing your arms; instead, let your loosely hanging arms be propelled by the emphasis of your waist turns. Though you allow your arms to go limp, leaving the propulsion of the swing to the turning of the waist, there is still a subtle measure of control that you exert. As you are turning toward the left, your right arm rotates clockwise, allowing the right palm to lightly tap your body in front at the end of your twist. Your left arm rotates subtly clockwise, allowing the back side of your left hand to tap the rear of your body.

Turning to the right side produces the opposite effect. If you are properly relaxed, this subtle clockwise and counterclockwise rotation of the arms occurs naturally as the arms are swinging and your body is turning from side to side. Power Standing, Heaven's Palms and Wet Noodles are considered the Trilogy of internal exercises in the DAIA Method. If nothing else, the three should be practiced all together, performing them one after the other with no breaks in between. You will find even more extensive explanation of this trilogy in the book, Opening the Energy Gates to Your Body Qigong by Bruce Frantzis. The author, an internationally known Qigong and Tai Chi master, among other internal and external martial arts, explains this trilogy of movements in minute detail, breaking them down into both body and energy mechanics.

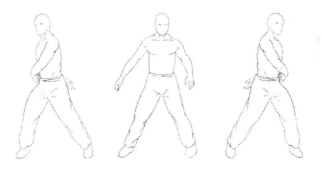

Chapter 5 - Globe Circles For Strong, Supple Neck Muscles

At some point in your life, for one reason or another, you may experience neck pain. This pain could result from a variety of reasons. In many cases people who sit improperly or for long periods of time, most notably hunched over a keyboard, often complain of neck pain. Many people slouch on the sofa while being entertained by hundreds of cable or satellite channels. The muscles that support the body are weakened by long periods of such laxity.

Performing the Trilogy of internal exercises normally alleviates such pain as body alignment is adjusted. Adding Globe Circles, which are stretching exercises, strengthens your neck muscles while also contributing to your neck's flexibility. Prevention of repetitive motion injuries is another benefit of this exercise. Performing Globe Circles at a slow pace may improve your neck's range of motion as bending forward, backward and side to side are inherent within the circles. Thus, the neck is stretched in all directions. In this step, do the Globe Circles only to the point where you can feel your neck stretch. Don't move your neck in a way that causes additional pain. While performing these important neck-stretching exercises, your breathing should be consistent with that shown in Power Standing. As explained, breathing properly helps relax muscles. Relaxed muscles are able to stretch farther and benefit more from exercise. Should you encounter or already have serious neck pain, do not attempt this exercise! Always roll your head to the point you feel the slightest pain, and then back off slightly.

Stand with the feet shoulder-width apart and your arms relaxed by your sides. Let your head gently tilt forward. Begin rotating slowly toward the left, and continue this rotation in the same direction for ten rotations. Repeat the opposite way. When rotating the head, do not put too much pressure on your neck during the backward rolls. Tilt your head back just as far as you would if you were gargling or drinking from a bottle. It is important not to force the neck backward. In doing this and all of the steps in this book, be aware of your body, and stay within a comfortable range of movement.

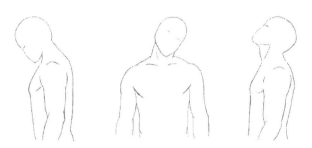

Chapter 6 - Develop Centrifugal Force with Center Circles

In addition to helping to loosen and relax the waist and lower back muscles, Center Circles develops centrifugal force and gives the kidneys a gentle massage. The kidneys are basically a two-unit filtration system, with one unit located on each side of your lower back. The kidneys are responsible for removing toxins from the blood after body cells have extracted vital oxygen and nutrients.

One of the most important areas of your body, the waist controls more than just the coordination of upper and lower body. It is the location of all the nerves that affect the total body's actions and stability. The waist is the source of movement of the shoulders, back, hips, knees, and feet. The rotational effect of Center Circles on the muscle groups in this area stimulates, develops, and empowers the function of the nerves, thereby improving mobility, flexibility and coordination. This is one of the main reasons why, for example, Tai Chi places such importance on waist training. A style of Chinese martial arts called Drunken Boxing depends eighty percent on waist action. This makes it vitally important to develop the waist to its fullest potential.

Accordingly, Center Circles is so-named because the center of a person is the midsection or the waist, and via the hip-crease connects the body's trunk. This area, in addition to synchronizing the body's movements, is the location of a meridian point where vital energy is created and stored. In meditation arts like Qigong, and martial arts like Tai Chi Chuan, the emphasis is on the rotation of the waist so that this energy will release from this meridian point and, controlled by the mind, as explained in an earlier chapter, begin to circulate within your body. Waist rotation is the catalyst for energy transmission and benefits the practitioner exponentially. The waist is your center. It is a major joint that controls and unifies all movements and transmission of power.

To perform Center Circles, place your palms on either side of your waist, palms covering each kidney. Your fingertips touch the spine, and the middle finger of each hand makes contact with the middle finger of the other hand. Begin rotating slowly at the waist, left to right, for ten rotations as shown in the illustration. Repeat the exercise in the opposite direction. Once again, do not let your head wobble. The head and upper body remains steady. Only the waist area is circling. As you perform this exercise, the tips of your fingers are providing a mini-massage to that area around the lower spine, further stimulating blood flow. The massage may also help relieve chronic pain in the lower back area. Because you've completed the Trilogy of internal exercises, energy was transmitted to your palms and fingertips. So as you are performing this exercise with your palms surrounding each kidney, and your fingertips centered on your spine, this chi energy flows into your lower back area, providing the healing needed.

Chapter 7 - Put Your Hips in Orbit

As we all know, tight hip muscles may make you more prone to injury. As well, tight hips may contribute to low back pain. The previous exercise improves circulation, gives you more flexibility, increased range of motion, and strengthens your hips as well as your buttocks and thighs. In addition to those that rotate the hips internally many muscles are required for the movement of your hips. Poor posture can severely compromise—pulling your toes, knees and lower back out of alignment— muscles that internally rotate the hips. Poor posture in your hips and spine when you stand or sit, (such as sitting with your knees turned in) can undermine internal hip rotation. Over time, as your body adapts to this posture, it causes the connective tissues in your hips and inner thighs to pull toward the midline of your body. Your hip rotators control both external and internal hip rotation in the femoral joint and the deepest layers of the hips beneath your buttocks. These rotators are the external and internal obturators, superior and inferior gemellus, piriformis and quadratus femoris. They all work together with adjacent muscles to produce movement and stabilize your hip joints to prevent injury. Those muscles, the gluteus medius, the anterior fibers of the gluteus minimus (abductors), and tensor fasciae latae (TFL) can become tight making it difficult to internally rotate your hips. Although the gluteus maximus—the main hip flexors along with piriformis on the back of the hips and the quadriceps at the front of the thighs that give you the ability to flex the hips and sit— is the largest of the gluteal muscles and one of the strongest muscles in the human body, they are subject to atrophying through constant pressure and neglect, such as constantly sitting for long periods.

As you age, joints tend to stiffen, become less limber, and more brittle. Range of motion may be inhibited by not enough movement, i.e., a couch potato, and not keeping fit. However, despite your age, people often experience tightness in the hips, and find their flexibility decreases as time passes. According to the American Chiropractic Association Rehab Council, stretching the hip rotator helps maintain not just the hip joint health, but spine health and walking function as well.[3] Your body uses less energy to move when your body is in alignment.

Performing Hips in Obit, is beneficial if you have tight hips. This exercise reduces your risk of injury by alleviating pain and helping to loosen the muscles in this area, thereby improving your level of flexibility and helping to increase your range of motion. You will also, after a certain amount of time practicing this step, begin to notice a type of spiraling energy developing within. However, this is a special type of energy and certain advanced techniques must be introduced in order to actually control this energy.

Commitment to this on a daily basis keeps the hip joints lubricated and limber. The rotation in this exercise is the same as in Center Circles with the exception that the rotations will be much wider to benefit the lower body from the waist to the feet. Thus, as an

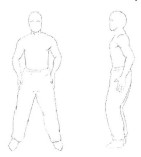

extension of Center Circles, Hips in Orbit, provides further benefits to the lower back.

Begin by opening the legs a little more than shoulder width apart. Cover each hip socket with your palms (see illustration) as you perform the rotations. Do not allow your upper body to tilt forward, backward, or wobble as your hips are in orbit.

---

[3] http://www.ccptr.org/index.php?s=hip+joint+

Chapter 8 - Rotate Knees

For centuries, Taoist monks practiced this step to promote physical and spiritual well-being. Energy from the upper body flows downward. Some of it is absorbed by the thighs. Since the knees are not load-bearing but load transference units designed to allow energy above to bypass them, sinking correctly, as taught in Power Standing, allows this transferred energy to be directed through the legs to the feet where the energy is dissipated into the ground.

The *Knee Rotation* here helps keep the knee joints lubricated and limber. This movement is a three-step process of sinking and rising while simultaneously rotating. The performance of this trilogy of movements helps strengthen the muscles, ligaments, and tendons that support your knee, and increases blood flow. Do not sink deeply, lift your heels off the ground, or allow your knees to extend beyond the boundary of your toes on the downward movement. Doing so puts undue pressure on the knees.

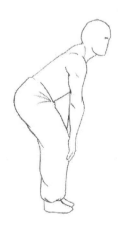

Move your feet approximately six inches apart. Inclining forward at the waist, keep the knees slightly buoyant and cover them with your palms. Briskly rub for about fifteen seconds until you feel warmth in your palms and knees. As your palms are covering your knees do not rest your weight there. Begin to slowly sink and rise as you rotate the knees left to right ten times. Repeat in the opposite right-to-left direction. Making this a lifestyle movement performed three to four times a week nurtures good maintenance and will allow you to have considerable range-of-motion indefinitely.

Chapter 9 - The Relaxing Way of Hill Climbing

This stretch is called the Hill Climbing Stretch. It requires you to take a large step to the side with your left foot—torso also turns toward the left. As you step, the left leg will fully bend while the right leg straightens with a slight bend. Ensure the bending of the left knee does not extend (bend) past the range of the toes. Doing so causes excessive pressure on the knee and could result in damage.

The slight bend in the right leg actually causes your leg muscles to constantly flex to keep balance. This pumps the blood, helping to maintain a constant flow. Again, as you are bending forward, ensure the bending knee *does not* move beyond the range of your toes. The rear foot is at an approximate thirty-five degree angle toward the forward foot. You may let your arms hang, place your hands on your hips, or rest them lightly on your leg (as shown in the illustration).

But, **do not lean on your leg** to rest your body weight there. The back of the straight leg is given a gentle stretch.

Hold the position for a minimum of 30 seconds before turning in the opposite direction to repeat for the right leg. Holding the position allows a gentle stretch. Do not bounce or try to force your legs to stretch past their normal range as they will naturally stretch, over time, without microscopic tearing of muscle fissures.

Chapter 10 - Leanin' on the Scene

To perform this exercise, take a large step to the side with your left foot—torso does not turn in the same direction as Hill Climbing Stretch. The left leg will be bent while the right leg remains straight but not locked stiff. As already explained, however, keep in mind that locked joints hinder maximum blood flow. Through its pumping action the heart generates pressure to pump blood throughout the body, down to the feet, and then back up to the heart. The heart, although powerful, still relies on the squeezing action of muscles in the legs to help push the blood back up the legs. However, locking your knees immobilizes the leg muscles, constricting the blood vessels. Blood can't return from the legs efficiently so blood pressure in the brain drops. Keeping the knees locked could actually lead to feeling dizzy or even fainting.

For each leg hold the position for at least 30 seconds. Do not bounce or try to force a longer stretch. Holding the position allows the sides of your leg to stretch gently from your foot to your groin area. Note that both feet face toward the front (see illustration) as you alternate the stretch on each leg. As above, your arms may hang loosely or you may place your hands on your waist.

Chapter 11 - Increase Your Stretch-a-bility

In this last exercise, your total lower body will enjoy a relaxing stretch from your hips to your toes. Sit with both legs straight in front of you as shown in the illustration. Do not press your legs down, as doing so will lock the knees. Keep the legs relaxed with a very slightly bend in the knees. While keeping your back straight, incline your body forward in an attempt to grab your ankles or toes. When performing this step, the shoulders have a tendency to shrug—tense up. If you continue to use the principle of Power Standing within this exercise you will be able to keep your shoulders relaxed while inclining forward and reaching toward your toes. Whether or not your hands can reach your feet, do not forcefully pull yourself forward in an attempt to get more stretch. Simply go to the point of resistance or where you feel slight discomfort, back off just a bit, and then hold it at that point for 30 to 60 seconds. If you can reach your ankles, lean forward only to the point of resistance, gently grab your ankles and hold it there. In performing this stretch it is vitally important not to arch your back because doing so will undermine your goal of stretching the spine and the hamstrings.

Keep the spine straight so that the benefit you receive is both a stretched spine and naturally stretched hamstrings. Do not bounce but relax in this position. It is known that some practitioners relax in this position for five minutes or more. Breathe deeply, not forcefully, as your leg muscles and spine each get a *gentle* stretch. Breathe fully into your lungs, and remember that the lower abdomen, not the chest, should expand upon inhaling. Breathing deeply will help supply essential oxygen to cells at the farthest parts of your body and will enable them to carry out their intended tasks.

The level of spine and hamstring flexibility one may obtain from this is short of amazing, as shown by this Taoist Qigong and Tai Chi master who performs this movement as one of his daily Qigong exercises. This ability, pulling the chin to the toes, comes with superb benefits but can only be achieved by consistent and diligent practice. Although you do not have to reach this level to be in excellent health, the benefit of attaining this level of mastery is worth the effort. "Add a millimeter to your tendons and add ten years to your life" is a Chinese Proverb expounding on the importance of stretching.

It is important to perform this movement in the mindset of Power Standing in order to have total body relaxation and change the nature of this movement. If you practice only the external form and pay no attention to self-cultivation and the internal aspect of this movement, you will experience some flexibility but you will be unable to translate this internally, which is what is necessary for achieving **internal stress release**.

Chapter 12 - Qigong's Relationship to Tai Chi

Overview of Qigong and Tai Chi

Qigong is more ancient in origin than Tai Chi. It is the over-arching, more original discipline. Qigong incorporates widely diverse practices designed to cultivate functional integrity and the enhancement of the life essence that the Chinese call Qi. Both Qigong and Tai Chi sessions incorporate a wide range of physical movements, including: slow, meditative, flowing, dance-like motions. In addition, they both can include sitting or standing meditation postures as well as either gentle or vigorous body shaking. Most importantly, both incorporate the purposeful regulation of both breath and mind coordinated with the regulation of the body. Qigong and Tai Chi are both based on theoretical principles that are inherent to traditional Chinese medicine (TCM).[1- References]

In the ancient teachings of health-oriented Qigong and Tai Chi, the instructions for attaining the state of enhanced Qi capacity and function point to the purposeful coordination of body, breath, and mind. Regulating breath and body clear the mind to "distill the Heavenly elixir within." This combination of self-awareness with self-correction of the posture and movement of the body, the flow of breath, and stilling of the mind, are thought to create a state which activates the natural self-regulatory (self-healing) capacity, stimulating the balanced release of endogenous neurohormones and a wide array of natural health recovery mechanisms which are evoked by the intended integration of body and mind.

Health-oriented Tai Chi and Qigong emphasize the same principles and practice elements. Given these similar foundations and the fashion in which Tai Chi has typically been modified for implementation in clinical research, we suggest that the research literature for these two forms of meditative movement should be considered as one body of evidence.

Qigong

Qigong translates from Chinese approximately, *to cultivate or enhance the inherent functional (energetic) essence of the human being*. It is considered to be the contemporary offspring of some of the most ancient (before recorded history) healing and medical practices of Asia. Earliest forms of Qigong make up one of the historic roots of contemporary Traditional Chinese Medicine (TCM) theory and practice.[2] Many branches of Qigong have a health and medical focus and have been refined for well over 5000 years. Qigong purportedly allows individuals to cultivate the natural force or energy ("Qi") in TCM that is associated with physiological and psychological functionality. Qi is the conceptual foundation of TCM in acupuncture, herbal medicine and Chinese physical therapy. It is considered to be a ubiquitous resource of nature that sustains human well-being and assists in healing disease as well as (according to TCM theory) having fundamental influence on all life and even the orderly function of celestial mechanics and the laws of physics. Qigong exercises consist of a series of orchestrated practices including meditation, breath practice, and body posture/movement, all designed to enhance Qi function (that is, drawing upon natural forces to optimize and balance energy within) through the attainment of deeply focused and relaxed states. From the perspective of Western thought and science, Qigong practices activate naturally-occurring physiological and psychological mechanisms of self-repair and health recovery.

Also considered part of the overall domain of Qigong is "external Qigong" wherein a trained medical Qigong therapist diagnoses patients according to the principles of TCM and uses "emitted Qi" to foster healing. Both internal Qigong (personal practice) and external Qigong (clinician emitted Qi) are seen as affecting the balance and flow of energy and enhancing functionality in the body and the mind. For the purposes of our review, we focused only on the individual, internal Qigong practice of exercises performed with the intent of cultivating enhanced function, inner Qi that is ample and unrestrained. This is the aspect of Qigong that parallels what is typically investigated in Tai Chi research.

There are thousands of forms of Qigong practice that have developed in different regions of China during various historic periods. They have been created by many specific teachers and schools. Some of these forms were designed for general health enhancement purposes and some for specific TCM diagnostic categories. Some were originally developed as rituals for spiritual practice. Others were designed to empower greater skill in the martial arts. An overview of the research literature pertaining to internal Qigong yields more than a dozen forms that have been studied as they relate to health outcomes (e.g., Guo-lin, ChunDoSunBup, Vitality or Bu Zheng Qigong, Eight Brocade, Medical Qigong).[2, 27–29]

The internal Qigong practices generally tested in health research (and that are addressed in this review), incorporate a range of simple movements (repeated and often flowing in nature), or postures (standing or sitting) and include a focused state of relaxed awareness and a variety of breathing techniques that accompany the movements or postures. A key underlying philosophy of the practice is that any form of Qigong has an effect on the cultivation of balance and harmony of Qi, positively influencing the human energy complex (Qichannels/pathways) which functions as a holistic, coherent, and mutually interactive system.

Tai Chi

Tai Chi translates to mean, *Grand Ultimate*. In the Chinese culture, it represents an expansive philosophical and theoretical notion which describes the natural world (i.e., the universe) in the spontaneous state of dynamic balance between mutually interactive phenomena including the balance of light and dark, movement and stillness, waves and particles. Tai Chi, the exercise, is named after this concept and was originally developed both as a martial art (Tai Chi Chuan or Taijiquan) and as a form of meditative movement. The practice of Tai Chi as meditative movement is expected to elicit functional balance internally for healing, stress neutralization, longevity, and personal tranquility. This form of Tai Chi is the focus of this review.

For numerous, complex sociological and political reasons,[2] Tai Chi has become one of the best known forms of exercise or practice for refining Qi and is purported to enhance physiological and psychological function. The one factor that appears to differentiate Tai Chi from Qigong is that traditional Tai Chi is typically performed as a highly choreographed, lengthy, and complex series of movements, while health enhancement Qigong is typically a simpler, easy to learn, more repetitive practice. However, even the longer forms of Tai Chi incorporate many movements that are similar to Qigong exercises. Usually, the more complex Tai Chi routines include Qigong exercises as a warm-up, and emphasize the same basic principles for practice, that is, the three regulations of body focus, breath focus and mind focus. Therefore Qigong and Tai Chi, in the health promotion and wellness context, are operationally equivalent.[†]

Note: See Reference page for References 1 – 35.

[†] http://www.ncbi.nlm.nih.gov/pmc/articles/PMC3085832

Tai Chi as Defined in the Research Literature

It is especially important to note that many of the RCTs investigating what is described as Tai Chi (for health enhancement), are actually not the traditional, lengthy, complex practices that match the formal definition of traditional Tai Chi. The Tai Chi used in research of both disease prevention and as a complement to medical intervention is often a "modified" Tai Chi (e.g., Tai Chi Easy, Tai Chi Chih, or "short forms" that greatly reduce the number of movements to be learned). The modifications generally simplify the practice, making the movements more like most health oriented Qigong exercises that are simple and repetitive, rather than a lengthy choreographed series of Tai Chi movements that take much longer to learn (and, for many participants, reportedly delay the experience of "settling" into the relaxation response). A partial list of examples of modified Tai Chi forms from the RCTs in the review are: balance exercises inspired by Tai Chi,[30] Tai Chi for arthritis, 5 movements from Sun Tai Chi,[31] Tai Chi Six Form,[32] Yang Eight Form Easy,[33,34] and Yang Five Core Movements.[34]

In 2003, a panel of Qigong and Tai Chi experts was convened by the University of Illinois and the Blueprint for Physical Activity to explore this very point.[35] The expert panel agreed that it is appropriate to modify (simplify) Tai Chi to more efficiently disseminate the benefits to populations in need of cost effective, safe and gentle methods of physical activity and stress reduction. These simplified forms of Tai Chi are very similar to the forms of Qigong used in health research.

For this reason, it is not only reasonable, but a critical contribution to the emerging research dialogue to review the RCTs that explore the health benefits resulting from both of these practices together, as one comprehensive evidence base for the meditative movement practices originating from China.[4]

---

[4] Jahnke R, Larkey L – A Comprehensive Review of the Health Benefits of Qigong and Tai Chi, Am. Journal of Health Promotion (AJHP), July/August 2010, Vol. 24, No. 6
http://healerwithinfoundation.org/wp-content/uploads/AJHP-Health-Benefits-of-QGTC-Jahnke.pdf

Chapter 13 – Your Daily Bank of Health
by Dr. Carl A. Totton, Psy.D

Human beings are creatures of habit.

A principle long recognized in psychology is that the best way to predict future behaviors is to look to past behaviors. Therefore, the only real way to institute change in one's life is to begin to practice different activities which then become new habits! This is the only certain way to change.

I've found that the best way to achieve this is to set a certain goal for a given amount of time. I like to use the 100-Day Method where you commit yourself to practice a given sequence of activities every day for one hundred days. This ensures that you have enough time to condition your neural pathways to establish a new habit which then becomes automatic. At that point it's easy. It's like putting money in a bank which gathers interest every single day, except here you are adding to your health account!

So, within the practice of daily standing meditation, here are some activities which will begin to change you at every level: mental, emotional, physical, energetic, behavioral, and spiritual! And, you'll be surprised at how simple it all really is, no particular background or state of health is required, and if you are currently unable to stand to perform these exercises, sitting is just fine. Try these for 100 days and change your life!

After 100 days of practice, you can simply repeat, or add or substitute some additional practices. Feel free to visit, www.WhatsThisTao.com and listen to my podcasts for more information about practices for natural living.

1. **Natural Standing and Breathing**

To begin, simply stand with your feet parallel and about shoulder width apart. Keep your knees slightly bent and in line with your toes. Allow your arms to just hang at your sides with a slight degree of roundness under your armpits. There is an acupuncture point for your heart meridian or pathway in the center of your armpits and this slight opening caused by the roundness allows a freer circulation of your heart's chi or energy.

Now, as you stand allow your body to completely relax. Imagine your head is suspended from the ceiling by a string so your head, neck, shoulders, and spine are in a naturally straight alignment. Don't bend or lean to the front, back, or sides. Use a mirror if possible to make sure your back is straight as some people cannot tell just by standing.

Next, allow your eyes to gently close. Breathe in and out of your nose gently while imagining that you have a balloon in your lower abdomen. As you inhale this balloon will slightly expand, and as you exhale it will release. With each breath imagine you are actually breathing pure energy up from the center of the earth and down from the heavens (the sun, stars, and moon). This will connect you to nature so you can have the feeling of becoming one with all of nature.

Finally, rather than feel you are experiencing all of this activity from your brain, move your awareness to a place known as the sacred space within your heart, a place of unity consciousness deep within the center of your heart (unlike the brain which is naturally polarized and divisive). Just imagine where this place is and you will naturally remember how to find it! All things in nature naturally tend to return to their original source. Please visit www.HeartofTao.com for additional guidance about heart centered meditation.

Now here are some simple daily exercises to perform that will have you smiling and feeling great as you release your stress.

2. Creating your Inner Smiles

As you continue to stand, bring you palms together facing up. Find out which of your palms feels the best on top, and allow your thumbs to touch slightly. Your hands will be at about the height of your lower abdomen just below your navel in a naturally relaxed posture. In the system of chi kung or qigong I teach, this area is called the lower tan tien (don tee-en), or field of elixir. Watch a dynamic video and additional details about chi kung instruction at www.heartoftao.com

Now, imagine that you can actually see inside of your body. Pretend that you can see your internal organs such as your heart, lungs, spleen, kidneys, gall bladder, bladder, pancreas, stomach and intestines. Then, in your imagination, put a little smiley face on each of these organs and simply watch how they look as they all smile at each other! Feel the inner sense of joy and peace this brings to you as you add a smile to your own face and smile along with the rest of your body. Let these smiles now spread to every part of your body like the blood cells, muscles, tissues, bones, nerves, tendons, and ligaments.

Share the wealth!

That's it! Just smile and let the rest simply take care of itself. Internally your brain wave activity will begin to shift to a more relaxed rhythm, your heart rate, pulse, and blood pressure will likely begin to drop and normalize, and your muscles, joints, and other bodily systems will begin to feel much more comfortable and will tend to release any previously painful sensations. You will soon notice your mind, emotions, breath, and energy begin to deeply relax and start to feel more energized and receptive. This is true wealth you are adding to your Bank of Health. You can't buy this kind of health but through this simple practice you can earn it.

3. The Picture of Perfect Health

You may have heard that you are what you eat. Well that's true and near the end of this book, you'll find much more information about natural diets and nutrition. But, it's also true that you are what you think! Many people seem to go through life with an abundance of negative thoughts in their heads most of the day. We worry about finances, relationships, what others are saying or thinking, our jobs, families, politics, our past and our futures, and on and on forming a mountain of worry. Enough! We need to learn to release these if we are going to be able to live in the present and find contentment.

So, again simply just stand with your palms resting together as before. Relax while taking several deep relaxing breaths and imagine with each exhalation that all tension is simply leaving your body. Then, in your imagination, visualize your body at its absolute peak of perfect health with perfect functioning in every system. See your circulatory, nervous, endocrine, respiratory, lymphatic, muscular, digestive, reproductive, skeletal, and immune systems as the picture of perfect health. If there was a time in your past where you were in much better health than now, see and feel that image as well.

Furthermore, in your mind, look ahead to the future when you will be at your absolute peak of health. Now, using all of your powers of imagination, see this vision of yourself as an incredibly healthy person standing right in front of you like a hologram facing the same way you are. Open your eyes and take a step or two until you have stepped right into this picture of perfect health and have put it on like a suit of clothes! Now it's you; you have become what you've created. Now feel it, feel what it's like to embody this image of perfection and know that this is now your new identity, your new reality.

Remember, you can't buy this level of health, but you can earn it.

4. Positive Imagery for Life and Health

Every day, just before you fall asleep and right after you awake, you have a window of opportunity to encode some positive practices which will begin to change your life. So again, while either standing as pictured above, or sitting or even when lying down, be sure to practice the following:

a. The Yes Set

As mentioned previously, many individuals move through life plagued by negative thinking. The solution is the Yes Set! Every day just say to yourself loudly (but just in your mind) YES!!! Say it over and over, YES, YES, YES, YES, YES! Combine this with the Inner Smiles and your life will change for sure! Do this morning, noon, and night, in fact any time you need a boost of positive energy. Just say YES!

b. Thank you, I love You!

There is a Hawaiian method of living and problem-solving called Ho'oponopono. This system maintains that if we take one hundred percent responsibility for what happens to us, we will lead far more fulfilling lives than if we place responsibility elsewhere, blame others, or feel like "poor me," etc. We also need to address our unconscious holding of patterns of tension and excessive data by releasing and letting it all go. How all this is accomplished is remarkably simple.

Morning, noon, and night, in fact all of the time, simply say to yourself and to your subconscious inner child, "Thank you, I love you!" That's it, what could be simpler? Just imagine that all day long you are feeling gratitude and love for yourself which then spreads to all of your other thoughts, feelings, behaviors, and attitudes. And, since we are each actually connected to all others within our energetic field through a form of quantum entanglement, what affects our thoughts and energies may very well start to affect others too. As you improve you may notice that others around you do so as well. Life is an inside job and as my Ho'oponopono teacher Dr. Ihaleakala Hew Len always says, "Have you ever noticed that when there's a problem you're always there?"

So by taking 100% responsibility for changing whatever shows up in our lives, we can reclaim our ultimate freedom and free will as the designer of our own destiny. Then, remarkably we can download pure inspiration from our own higher selves after we've essentially cleaned our conscious and subconscious of all of the debris that was in our way. Change how you hold reality and you'll change your life!

c. A Safe Place

As a psychologist, I work with many individuals who have led traumatic and unfulfilled lives. I also work with highly successful people who simply wish to perform even better and maximize their abilities in business, sports, family life, and all other life activities. This is known as peak performance or flourishing. Come visit me at, www.DrCarlTotton.com for more information about creating optimal functioning and peak performance. An exercise that allows each person to reach their peak whether coming from a more dysfunctional or more comfortable background is the Safe Place. Here's how to do it:

As you stand with your palms resting together as shown above, relax and allow your eyes to close while breathing slowly and rhythmically. Now, imagine you are in a beautiful place within nature: a beach or an island, perhaps the desert looking at the stars, in a forest or a meadow or a beautiful garden, someplace where you know you'd feel great. It can be a place you've visited before or a place you've seen pictures of and always wanted to visit.

As you imagine this special place, use all of your senses to truly experience it as real. Smell the flowers, feel the wind or sun on your skin, hear the relaxing sounds of nature like birds chirping or a relaxing surf or water fountain; in other words, totally experience yourself in this remarkably beautiful and special location. This is your *Safe Place*.

Now, feel your breathing relax and deepen as your mind just lets go while drifting and floating as if on a cloud. Feel a smooth wave of complete relaxation move throughout your entire body from head to toe as if you've just had the world's greatest massage. Let your mind, body, breath, emotions and energy all slide into a dream-like state where you feel completely safe and well taken care of. Now, in this state, do any planning you need to accomplish, any problem-solving or projects you need to attend to, even go back and observe any previous events or activities where you wish you could have altered the outcomes. Envision the episodes moving towards a more satisfying conclusion as you observe from your Safe

Place. Learn to give yourself a daily vacation as your mind and imagination simply soars to new heights of joy, serenity, and peace. That's it!

Conclusion

Now that you've become familiar with creating your daily bank of health, a word about practicing. As I mentioned at the beginning of this chapter, we are conditioned by our habits. Take control of your life by instituting some of the standing meditation exercises above into your daily life. Perhaps you'd like to do the first and second exercises in the mornings, then the third and fourth at night, or the reverse, it's up to you. Just determine that you will do them for the next 100 days for sure. Keep a journal where you keep track of this daily regimen marking off each day as you progress. Note however, if you miss a day you need to return to the beginning and start the 100 days over! But that's ok; each practice session is more life in your bank of health! Our lives can occur by accident or by design, the choice is yours. If you learn to use all that you've been given and approach life as an opportunity to learn and grow, then you can live a fulfilled life where how you feel inside is matched by the external world you will begin to attract. This law of attraction happens when your mind, emotions, and body are all in alignment with the deepest desires of your heart. And, as you increase your happiness, you'll find that this is contagious and others lives will elevate to join with yours. In spite of any setbacks caused by things not within your control, you will experience peace and contentment, able to accept the things you cannot change while experiencing to the fullest those which you can. Instead of being a victim of your fate your will become the creator of both a better future and a present life where you are living fully. Always remember, the choice is yours. Choose wisely and you will become wealthy beyond all measure within your Bank of Health!

Dr. Carl Allen Totton is a clinical psychologist, professor, Taoist Priest, martial arts grandmaster, and shamanic energy healer. He is the founder and director of the Taoist Institute in North Hollywood where he teaches many traditional Chinese martial, healing, meditative, and spiritual arts. He has trained in the martial arts since 1963 and taught in the same location since 1981. He is the co-editor of the book, Kenpo Continuum, volume 2., which may be found at www.Amazon.com

Dr. Totton has taught at five colleges and universities, including two schools of Traditional Oriental Medicine. He was inducted into the Martial Arts History Museum and United States Martial Arts Halls of Fame, and is listed in over twenty volumes of Who's Who biographies, including Who's Who in America and Who's Who in the World. His doctoral dissertation in clinical psychology from Pepperdine University examined meditation as an altered state of consciousness, and looked at ways to maximize the therapeutic benefits of meditation and mindfulness.

His martial arts background includes training in Chinese and American Kenpo, Kung Fu, Limalama, Kajukenbo, Tai Chi Chuan (Yang, Chen, Wu, & Guang Ping styles), Hsing-I Chuan, Pa Kua Chang, Lu Ho Ba Fa (Water Boxing), Aikido, and Arnis. He has received direct private instruction from the pioneering martial arts instructors Ark Yuey Wong, Share K. Lew, SGM Edmund K. Parker, Haumea Lefiti, Tino Tuiolosega, John Leoning, Remy Presas, Doo Wai, John Fey, Ralph Shun, York Why Loo, and Chen Xiaowang, among others.

Within the Chinese martial arts community, Dr. Totton has long been known as "The Keeper of the Flame" as he is a martial arts historian and keeper of ancient traditions. He has an extensive martial arts library with numerous hard to obtain and out-of-print books, many of them signed by their authors: this includes books signed by martial arts luminaries like O-Sensei Uyeshiba, Gogen Yamaguchi (The Cat), and Ed Parker.

He owns thousands of martial arts magazines including every issue of Black Belt and Inside Kung Fu magazines, among others. As a Board Certified Holistic Health Practitioner, his office is filled with healing herbs from around the world, many of which he concocted himself. As the "Master to the Masters" he is often consulted by other instructors when they have questions. Next door to his school is his Taoist Temple for spiritual training and healing.

Dr. Totton is the founder of **The Core System**, www.TaoistInstitute.com/store, a new method of integrating the ancient roots of the traditional healing, spiritual, and martial arts and transforming them for contemporary applications. His favorite quotation comes from Dr. Charles Richet, winner of the Nobel Prize in Medicine: "*I didn't say it was possible. I only said it was true.*"

Many times there are the skeptics that doubt the validity of the health-transforming and healing modalities of the traditional healing arts or so-called alternative medicine. However, there is substantive evidence for the efficacy of these methods, as Dr. Totton has used a variety of these methods over the years such as, Medical Chi Kung, Reiki, Tui Na or Jin Shin Do acupressure massage on his mother, a Centenarian of 101 years old! It appears to have worked well! Her physician always tells her, "Whatever you're doing just keep doing it!" Dr. Totton's mother, Elva Totton, was born in Oklahoma in 1914, and the photo was taken in September 2015 on her 101'st birthday. She still lives in her own home in Los Angeles with a caregiver. She retired as a pre-school teacher and remains in good health!

Chapter 14 – Yixingong - Standing Like a Tree For Strength, Health and Longevity
by John P. Painter PhD ND

"In the end whatever you call it; it is no more than the mind and the breath becoming as one. It is simply the Yin and the Yang influenced internally with their spirit energy entwined."

- Master Wei, Boyang "Can Tong Qi" AD 142

As a young sickly boy growing up in East Texas one of the great gifts I was given from my teacher of Li family Way of Life Force Boxing (Daoqiquan) was his version of a standing at post practice (Zhang Zhuang). Master Li, Long-dao who's forte was Baguazhang called this method, intention palm (Yi-zhang). Today after years of research, medical study and consultation with many grand masters I have changed the name of his standing method to Intention Heart Skill (Yixingong). The term refers to mind intent (YI) combined with heart mind or attitude (Xin) developed as a skill (Gong) in other words using mind and heart skill.

At The Gompa Center in Arlington Texas my research team and I have devoted years to investigating the methods of Li, Long-dao's standing practice. With the aid of experts in bio-mechanics, humankinetics, neurology and physiology and psychology we have updated both the explanations and training methods to allow students a better understanding of the science behind this practice.

Now we have updated and created Yixingong to show you exactly how to produce the amazing benefits of standing practice through the use of special imaging exercises that activate the skeletal system, nervous system, endocrine systems, blood and lymph circulation and muscular systems in a way that works harmoniously to produce a calm mind glowing health and increased longevity. This is not mystical pseudo-science. Properly taught and practiced you will be able to feel the effects in a very short time if you understand and follow our instructions.

Yixingong Advanced Principles

What makes Yixingong different from standard traditional Chinese practices of standing exercise / Zhan Zhuang is that we do not emphasize non-scientific theories or focus on Qi development except where it is linked to correct breathing methods. There is no emphasis on meridian circulation or pseudo-science. Yixingong draws from the first master of Chinese healing modalities Wei Boyang, quoted above, who also said, *"The Mind Commands, The Body Responds and The Result (Qi) follows."* Therefore we place strong emphasis on learning to use the mind to control the body through a process of developing a heightened sensitivity to ones internal and external environment.

Yixingong makes use of imagery and sense memories to improve circulation of blood and lymphatic fluids and to improve the functioning of the neurological system for increased strength, speed and reaction time. To fully understand this concept would take a large volume of hundreds of pages. The best I can do here is to give a general overview of these methods in hopes that my efforts may be of some benefit to the reader.

Does It Work

All indications and research point to the efficacy of this method. From personal experience as a young sickly boy who was given a death sentence by doctors to be executed before the age of 20, I have beaten the odds and then some. Today at 70 years of age I am healthy and full of energy, often running rings around my 20 and 30 year old students. I am also cold- and flu- free for 30 years with a full (but slightly receding) head of dark brown hair and supple skin tone. Then there are the hundreds of testimonials from current and former students attesting to the usefulness of the methods for all manner of complaints. But, don't believe me; try it and be the judge for yourself.

Six Core Principles of Yixingong

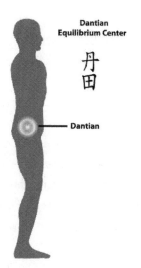

1. Find Structure

Structure refers to you posture. It is the way you align your joints in the arms, legs and spine so as to be capable of allowing the whole body to work as a single unit to produce maximum force with minimal effort. This is known in the internal and external martial arts as Whole Body Power (Zhengti-jin). Included in finding structure is also finding your center of control or balance. In China the term for the location of this center is called the cinnabar field (Dantian) located in the center of the pelvic region at approximately three inches below the umbilicus.

This imaginary point is actually the center of balance for the human body. Learning to move, walk, sit or act from this point aids in the achievement of physical and emotional balance.

2. Learn Song

Relaxation of the muscles with dynamic stability while retaining muscle tonus is called relaxing forces (Song-Jin) and is necessary for success in standing. Tense muscles create stress in the mind-body feedback loop diminishing quick response times in emergency situations. Tension also prevents flow of blood, lymph and innervation from easily functioning. Simply put, all postures used in standing practice must contain a high state of relaxation to a level that any lesser tension used to hold the posture would result in the arms or body collapsing. Just enough and no more is the key to feeling relaxed internal energy. Each posture must be examined to find this relaxing force.

4. Train non-localization

After achieving relaxation ability (Song-Jin) the student begins the next phase of training, non-localization (Meiyou Fenhua) in which the center point (Dantian) is mentally expanded internally so the entire body becomes the center point. This prevents investing tension or strength in any one location within the body. Localization of mind in any one place is a mistaken process which prevents the use of whole body awareness and power. Various images selected by the student may be used to produce the feeling of whole body integration. This is a process know as non-differentiation or non-localization.

5. Develop Guided Imaging Skill

Guided imagery (*Chengxiang*) is the true gateway to using any power, strength or speed development or healing modality in standing. For best results imagery (Chengxiang) must be coupled with relaxation skills (Song-Jin) when training with Yixingong. Guided imagery is used during Quiet Sitting meditation and standing training to stimulate various functions of the external and core muscle groups responsible for aiding in healing, circulation of blood, lymph, and producing increases in the quality of movement, strength and speed. Imagery increases in affect in relation to the levels of relaxation skills.

6. Retrain the Nervous System and Muscle Function

Using Guided imagery coupled with Song-Jin for martial art or sports applications we are actually using the mind to retrain muscle motor neurons in order to increase firing capabilities of skeletal muscle. This process works to increase muscle fiber hypertrophy thus improving strength potential and speed capabilities. Guided imagery used in this way is believed to change or influence the capacity of stabilizer muscle fibers (Slow Twitch) normally used to maintain joint stability and balance to function as if they were mobilizer muscle fibers (Fast Twitch). Yixingong training has been shown to help recruit muscle stabilizer fibers within the functioning mobilizers enabling them to support the mobilizer fibers during the production of force thereby adding to the power of each individual muscle group through increased contraction capabilities. Imagery also has been shown to improve muscle function, strength, size and speed. The interesting point is that to achieve this type of power with the mind during training one must be in a state of profound relaxation (Song-jin) and not moving while visualizing moving against a high level of resistance from outside the body. In other words feel as if moving a resistance but do not tense the external muscles used in the imagined action.

Guided Imagery For Health, Fitness and Martial Training

While it is generally believed that imagining oneself as being faster or stronger to enhance performance is relatively a new idea we can find examples dating back thousands of years of individuals using imagery throughout Chinese health and martial arts training. Since ancient times primitive tribes, shamanistic healers and martial artists have imagined themselves becoming ferocious animals or elements of nature through a process of visualization or mental imagery.

As we move into understanding the visualization or imaging process we should begin by defining the word imagination. Imagination is whatever is occurring in your mind not directly caused by what you are experiencing from the outside world. If you look at a tree, what you see is not an "image;" you are seeing a real tree. But when the tree is not there, and you picture it in your mind, then you are producing an image from your stored memory of the tree. These images or sensations are called sense memories (Gan Jue Ji Yi). Normally "imagination" is not truly imagery as it refers to imaging things or events that don't exist except in your "imagination" for example, dragons.

Your mind has the ability to see in three specific ways (1) observation of external real objects in real time, (2) A memory of visualized real objects as images in your mind, and (3) visualized imaginary objects in your mind. Each of these three ways of seeing involves imagery, because in all cases you are seeing something or sensing something, and "seeing" is a mental event, happening in your mind. When a person cannot tell whether he or she is seeing, smelling, tasting or touching a real object or just imagining it this is a hallucination.

This ability to activate guided imagery is one of the most powerful concepts for health or ill health in the world. Science has shown clearly that what you think is what you become and what you think or desire affects your health and longevity, speed, strength and healing potential. The process of guiding your thoughts into the body moves from the conscious mind into the unconscious control centers of the brain that controls all aspects of the sympathetic and Para-sympathetic nervous system. It can even affect the immune system and the growth or dissolution of cancers as proven by Dr. Carl Simonson in his landmark mind-body cancer research. This is the real science behind what traditional Chinese Medicine calls Qigong.

Below I have presented a series of basic methods for developing these concepts as found in our Yixingong methods. This training is derived from Li family arts and is by no means a complete manual on the practice. By training these simple methods on a daily basis it will be possible for your mind to awaken to its latent potential of influencing the body. Through this understanding you can enter the door of unlimited possibilities. To know more you may contact us through our website, www.TheGompa.com .

Yixingong

First Posture The Void

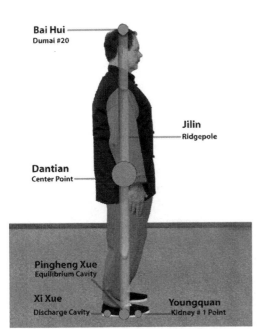

Creating a lasting, powerful image that produces a profound affect on health and physical performance is not an easy task. It requires training and an understanding of how the process works. A discussion of the different forms of imagery is in order here. For this ability is the real key to what many call life force skill (*Qigong*) and internal skill (*Nei-gong*)

The first posture, the void (*Wuji*) is the key to all standing forms Yixingong. It is in this shape that we begin to learn correct balance and body alignments. We should examine the basic positioning of the head, torso, legs and feet, as it will be only the arms that assume other positions while the head and body do not change during other standing forms.

Shown in the accompanying photo are the main points of balance and structure. During all standing forms training the Ridgepole (*Jilin*) from the Center point (*Dantian*) to the Crown of the head point (*Bai Hui*) must be correctly aligned as if it were a bamboo rod planted in the earth and ascending to the sky. While in this posture it is important to find dynamic relaxation or (song-jin). One image I use is of my spine being a flexible rod of bamboo and my body as a nice soft leather coat hanging effortlessly on the rod. The bamboo pushes my crown (Baihui) upward and my hips and pelvis feels as if sinking into the earth below. Also beginners do not stand on the Kidney #1 point. Stand with weight in the center of the foot on the point know as the Equilibrium Cavity or Taiji point.

Once this ability is achieved you can begin using the selected visual or sensory imagery of your choice for the practice. In the case of sore muscles or injuries to joints you might use a sense memory of thick warm water soothingly running down all sides, front and back of your body washing away the pain. You can create an illusory image of a warm compress on sore joints or muscles. In time you will begin to notice the warmth growing in proportion to your imaging skills. With a little imagination you can learn to focus these skills into muscles and internal organs to improve blood, lymph and Qi flow to the area. If you have trouble imagining the water image, go stand in a warm shower and develop a good sense memory to use in your practice.

Begin by standing in the Void posture for a minimum of 15 minutes a day to find the correct body alignments (structure); then proceed to developing the relaxation ability (Song-jin) by consciously releasing any areas of unnecessary tension or tightness. Next you can begin to use the mind to influence health, vitality, speed and power. Unlike traditional standing methods, marathon standing, holding postures for an hour at a time are not necessary for Yixingong training.

Second Posture Hold The Ball

Once the principles of The Void are understood and goals achieved you move into the next phase of training known as holding the ball.

Holding the Ball
Finding Song
Phase 1

Finding Song

To achieve this posture raise your arms with a gentle curve at the elbow of both arms, relax your wrists and fingers. The arms should be slightly bowed on the inside as if you were holding a large bubble gently so it presses on the chest, arms and palms. Visualize a huge soft bubble supporting your arms. Allow them to feel as if sinking into the bubble, but do not allow them to move. You should try to keep them in this position using the least amount of energy possible. Notice the difference when the arms are stiff and when they release tension; this is finding the Song-jin in the posture. When you can move into this posture and feel the release of unnecessary tension almost as soon as you come to the position it is time to move to the next phase of holding the ball.

Holding The Ball Phase 2

Hold the ball posture (Zhiqiu) should be the second position you train in Yixingong standing. Here you will maintain the ridgepole and balance yourself over the center of your feet. At first in this position you hold the posture as if clasping a round sphere in your arms, elbows relaxed and hanging downward. Test your imaging or sense memory skills by pretending you are gently squeezing the ball and notice if you can feel even the slightest presence of the illusory sphere.

As you skill improves you will be able to sense the ball's presence and even feel as if it were pushing or inflating against your arms and chest. This is a good experiment to improve your imaging skills. Imagine the ball inflating and deflating and feel push apart or draw your arms in or out.

If you have trouble with this ability then develop a real sense memory by holding a large balloon or Swiss exercise ball between your arms and squeeze it as shown in the photo. Do this a number of times then put the ball down and recreate the sensation with your memory.

In time it will be become easy to sense the presence of your imaginary ball. This is an indication that your sense memory or mind over body skills are improving and you are on the road to truly understanding the power of the mind and its influence on the body both inside and out.

Third Posture Hand Float in Water

Here we ramp up the training by adding in the second exercise which is called the Dynamically Opposing Force sensation (Dongtai duli lilang)

Fig 1 Find Song

Fig. 1 Phase one: Hands float posture (Shou Piaofu) is the third position in Yixingong standing. Here you will maintain the ridgepole and balance yourself over the center of your feet. At first in this position you hold the posture as if your palms were resting on the tops of two very soft globes or balloons, elbows and shoulders are relaxed and hanging downward. Visualize the huge bubbles supporting your arms. Allow them to feel as if sinking into the bubble, but do not allow them to move. You should try to keep them in this position using the least amount of energy possible. Notice the difference when your arms are stiff and how they feel when you release tension; this is finding the Song in the posture.

Fig 2 Push **Down & Forward**

Fig. 2 Phase Two: Imagine pressing two air filled balls down in a pool of water. Keep the balls steady and not allow them to slip from under your hands. Mentally press downward and forward on the imaginary balls. Remember do not tense any muscles during the exercise. Feel the lifting up sensation in your arms created by the balls resisting your efforts. The imaginary balls make your torso feel as if it is being pushed upward. To counteract this create a downward sensation in your torso and legs as if sinking against the upward pressure. At the same time feel your legs trying to straighten against the resistance of the two spheres. Remember to remain in Song-jin. All sensations and feelings occur at the same time throughout the entire body.

Fig 3 Push & Expand

Fig. 3 Phase Three: Here you practice the same exercise as in phase two and then add a feeling of the body's energy expanding like a sphere in 360°; this is called the Golden Sphere (Jinhuang Qiuxing). Allow this feeling to surround you during the exercise. You can control the imaginary sphere to feel as if it is closing in on you and you have to expand it while pressing the balls into the water with a forward and downward action.

Attempting to add this layer before you are ready may cause you to loose the Phase two energy. Work on this until you can create both feeling easily.

When you can attain these goals your ability to use your intention (yi) to control your body will have greatly improved and you will be ready to enter the gate of true internal energy. Then you will understand, *"In the end whatever you call it; it is no more than the mind and the breath becoming as one."*

Personal Experience Standing Heals Torn Biceps Muscle

Author Showing Results of Yixingong Biceps Repair Experiment

Some years ago it was my misfortune to be involved in a martial arts application that resulted in a partial tear of my right biceps muscle. After the accident I was told that without surgery I would be unable to curl more than ten to fifteen pounds with my right arm. At the time, because of my profession, insurance was a very expensive luxury. As we could not pay for an operation; I was left with a barely usable right arm.

Remembering the research of exercise physiologist, Dr. Guang Yue, at the Cleveland Clinic Foundation in Ohio, who found that mentally visualizing exercise movements in relaxed muscle tissue was enough to increase strength in muscle fibers, I began a highly disciplined regimen of our Yixingong imagery to heal the injury.

Dr. Yue's work showed that one can increase muscle strength solely by sending a larger signal to motor neurons from the brain into relaxed muscle tissue. I began each morning with Yixingong void standing during which I visualized the blood vessels of the arm sending fresh nutrient rich blood into the damaged biceps. I also visualized individual muscle fibers lengthening and becoming thicker and stronger. All the while I was standing relaxed in song-jin arms hanging loosely by my side. No flexing or tension was allowed to enter the arms during the exercise.

For the first two weeks there appeared to be little or no sign of improvement, but having faith in my methods I persevered. During the third week my arm would begin to feel warm and I could see a noticeable color change in the upper arm as it flushed with blood during the Yixingong standing. As more mobility returned to the limb I continued with renewed resolve to heal my damaged biceps by this method. By the middle of the second month the atrophied biceps muscle seemed to be getting longer and a bit larger. To the amazement of my doctors the rather pronounced gap between the forearm and distal head of the biceps seemed to be decreasing. The muscle seemed to be lengthening; measurements taken by my physician of the muscles length and circumference confirmed that this was indeed the case.

My practice continued for three months until full mobility of the arm was regained. Only then did I begin performing resistance exercises with light cables and other exercises. Within a year and without surgery strength had returned to the muscle. In fact, my right biceps was actually larger and stronger than before the injury.

The gap from the tear in the right arm never completely filled in, but it is hardly noticeable and the arm is again fully functional. I had discovered that combining intention with visualization, self talk and exercise produces profound results at a neurological level. These findings although largely anecdotal imply that standing meditation can be a valuable adjunct to the development of physical speed, strength and power through the use of guided imagery techniques when coupled with internal type standing practice—at least in our Li family Yixingong methods.

Dr. John P. Painter PhD ND

The Gompa Center Arlington Texas

Dr. John P. Painter

John Painter began training in the Li family styles of Baguazhang, Taijiquan, Xingyiquan, and Daoist Qigong and Yoga in 1957. Painter studied with Shifu Li, Long-dao of Sichuan Province China until shortly after 1969 when he was provided with a letter of lineage naming him the inheritor of the Li family style in North America.

From 1970 to 1978 Painter worked as a professional Magician, Escape artist and actor entertaining from New York to Florida, and to the Magic Castle in Hollywood. It was during this time that he also worked in the off season as a professional bodyguard for film and television stars like Phil Donahue, Craig T. Nelson as well as the rich and famous of the Dallas Jet Set.

Painter has also appeared in three full length motions pictures as an actor. He has consulted and choreographed martial arts fight scenes for two films and numerous live performances. Painter has been interviewed on national television and written up in magazines like Vogue, Pa Kua Journal, Black Belt, Inside Kung Fu, National Star and many others promoting the internal arts.

During the 1980's Dr. Painter studied Tibetan Meditation and the Yantra method of Nyida Khajor Tibetan Yoga with numerous Tibetan Buddhist teachers and the venerable Trangu Rinpoche. Today Painter holds a Ph.D. in Chinese Naturopathic medicine He has been teaching Chinese internal martial arts and Qigong around the world for over 45 years. Dr. Painter was the owner and publisher of Internal Arts Magazine from 1986 to 1993 a magazine devoted to scientific research on Qigong and other Asian mind-body medical principles.

Dr. Painter instructs Baguazhang and Xingyiquan, Qigong, Daoist philosophy and Tibetan mind-body health and longevity courses at the Gompa Center in Arlington Texas. The Gompa is the oldest Chinese martial arts school in Texas. He also oversees a network of branch schools throughout the United States, Great Britain, Germany, Israel and Canada. Dr. Painter was elected to the Inside Kung Fu Hall of Fame, The Texas Martial Arts Hall of Fame and was named as one of the most sought after Chinese internal martial arts seminar instructors in America by Inside Karate and Black Belt magazines.

Dr. Painter is available for lectures, consultation, workshops, seminars or personal training by special appointment or at The Gompa Center. Visit www.TheGompa.com for complete info on all programs.

John P. Painter PhD ND
PO Box 1777
Arlington TX 76004
817-860-0129
TheGompa@aol.com
www.TheGompa.com

Chapter 15 – Nutrition: A Trilogy of Nourishment

The three prominent sources of nutrition the human body needs for maintainence and survival are: **air, water**, and **food** in that order. This forms an important trilogy of nourishment. All three work in unison 24/7 in the process of perpetually renovating a decaying body. If any one of the three pieces go missing it is virtually impossible for the body to thrive.

Chapter 1 touches on the trilogy of air, food, and water, with an emphasis on air, which is the most important of the three. Here in this chapter, let's take a closer view of water, to *home* in on the "why" of its importance, and the healing nature of food.

H_2O

Factually speaking, the majority of people on the planet **DO NOT** get enough fluids, i.e., plain, pure H_2O that allows the human body to operate at its peak. Nearly everyone is functioning at deficient levels. And, because of this the immune system is easily breached, allowing invading, harmful microorganisms to easily overpower the weak system and rapidly multiply practically unchallenged, bringing with it sundry symptoms of illness, especially a cold or the Flu.

Drinking enough fluids helps to maintain your body, which is primarily made up of water. On average, males are about 60% water and females are about 55% water.

Fluids—about 2 to 3 quarts of water every day—drain from the body 24/7: tears, vapor from the nose and mouth, urination, and sweat from the largest organ on your body–the skin, which covers you from head to toe in an unbroken, pliable form. The norm is to drink at least eight 8-ounce glasses of water a day. Athletes, people who live or work in hot environments, and people who perspire heavily lose more water and need to drink even more to keep up with the loss.

Yet many people are walking around in a mostly dehydrated state simply because, rather than to drink throughout the day, many believe that if they are not thirsty then they don't need to refuel. However, thirst is a poor indicator of fluid needs, especially as you age. Thirst is actually the body's warning signal that it has already began shutting down certain parts of the body which is why you may have itchy skin, dry eyes, a dry itchy scalp, brittle nails, falling hair, dry, cracked lips, a dry mouth, bad breath and a lack of energy, which may lead to low mental functioning and increase stress on the body.

The three rules of thumb when it comes to water are:

1. Drink twice as much as it takes to quench your thirst.
2. Drink Frequently throughout the day to prevent dehydration.
3. Drink at least eight glasses daily or one cup for every 20 pounds of body weight.

You can count fruit juices and bottled water in your tally. However, beverages such as coffee or alcohol have a mild diuretic effect, which promotes urination and therefore water loss. Green tea is another way to add fluids, and this beverage is chock-full of phytonutrients that may help lower your risk of developing cancer.

One way to ensure you have those eight glasses each day is to fill a pitcher with your allotment of water and keep it on your desk at work or on the kitchen table at home. You also can fill eight glasses and place them in a convenient spot out of the way, such as on the kitchen counter or dining room table. Your goal is then clearly marked, and that goal is reached when the pitcher or glasses are empty.

If you are a student, drink water between each class at school. The best indicator that you're drinking enough water is when your urine is pale yellow to clear. A dark yellow color is a sign your body is dehydrated and is concentrating the urine in an effort to conserve water.

Living in today's world, it is nearly impossible to avoid exposure to environmental pollutants: air and water pollution, food additives, second-hand smoke, and other toxins. When it comes to cleansing your body of harmful toxins, however, organic food and/or whole-food vitamins really is the best medicine. You'll be amazed to learn that many of your favorite fruits, vegetables, nuts, oils, and beans help ward off the harmful effects of contaminants and also cleanse the body's detoxification organs like the liver, intestines, kidneys, and skin, preventing harmful toxic buildup.

When you consistently eat the right foods in moderate quantities your body will return the favor with internal and external rejuventation. Though eating nutritiously will give you excellent health, adding a moderate amount of consistent exercises, making it a life-style will help maintain a youthful vigor well into your years as a senior citizen.

***DO NOT** wait until you are thirsty before drinking. Thirst is an indicator your body is dehydrated and severely under level. At this level to protect their integrity, internal organs, steal water from less important areas such as the skin. The average human body undergo much maltreatment due to lack of proper hydration.

Air provides this last but not least of the trilogy—food—with oxygen as it mixes with bodily fluids, beginning with the saliva produced by your mouth to start the process of breaking down solids into a simi-liquid state for transference to the stomach. This internal organ is where hydrodynamic and mechanical forces act on the ingested food and prepares it for release in the gastrointestinal (GI) tract. From the GI, the bioavailability of nutrients is quite abundant for use by the entire body. Consumption of the foods listed below are actually a very enjoyable way of obtaining the vital, energy-producing nutrients that keeps your body's organs, including the largest (the skin) running efficiently.

Food

Homegrown Medicinal Plants

You can save much money annually over what you pay for useless over-the-counter (OTC) medicines and drugs? And, many prescription medications are toxic chemicals that can potentially do more harm than good—just take a careful read of the label of your prescription medication and you'll see warnings of the damage they can cause you. By the way, please note very carefully, both OTCs and prescription meds **DO NOT** heal your body whatsoever. Pharmaceutical drugs have never healed anyone and has actually caused more deaths than you may realize. However, that damaging information is, of course, kept as much away from the public eye as possible so it won't crimp the multibillion dollar annual revenues of the pharmaceutical juggernaut.

With that stated, Coach Melvin introduces to you eight (8) highly medicinal plants you can grow in a small flower pot right at home. The effectiveness of these powerhouses are unmatched by OTCs, and nearly any expensive prescription, pharmaceutical drugs you can purchase.

Because growing medicinal herbs at home have a wealth of both nutritional and medicinal benefits, you will discover the joy in growing potted plants inside, on your balcony, or in your garden. It provides convenient access to many natural home remedies. Surprisingly, the following eight plants does not provide just a single medicinal benefit but are instrumental in providing healing to multiple illnesses.

Take lemon balm for example, did you know it may be used as a mosquito repellent, or even as a rinse aid in your laundry? You'll find out more below. So sit back in a comfortable place and enjoy reading about and taking note of how these eight powerful medicinal plants will positively enhance you health and your life.

Aloe Vera

Because Aloe Vera plants are very succulent and consist of 95% water, they are extremely frost tender. This plant grows with moist or well drained dry soil and under the sun. It has been used for a variety of ailments, and as an ointment for burns, cuts, and rashes, as well as an ingredient in various beauty preparations.

Peppermint

This popular medicinal herb is normally used to treat digestive issues, particularly to help with indigestion and upset stomachs. It is enriched with Vitamins A, Vitamin C and magnesium. Peppermint can be used in cooking too, it also helps to fresh your breath. You can grow peppermint both outdoors and indoors, and is very easy to grow.

Tea Tree

Tea tree oil is antibacterial, anti fungal and antiseptic. It can be used to treat many health problems, including chronic fatigue syndrome, fever, acne, vaginal infections, thrush, verrucae, insect bites, athlete's foot and burns. Even the Aborigines have been using the tea tree leaves for medicinal purposes, like chewing on young leaves to relieve headaches. (**For Texas, plant in October**)

Thyme

Thyme is excellent in treating congestion, indigestion, and coughs. It might even help with yeast **infections** and to **regulate** blood pressure levels. Thyme grows best from seedlings planted in a sunny spot, and it's easy to care of it.

Echinacea

Echinacea is a good plant for both internal and topical healing thanks to its antiviral and antibacterial properties. It's especially good for relieving allergies, treating wounds, burns and sores. It needs sunlight and well drained soil. Here's a link to 12 different ways Echinacea can heal you of various illnesses - www.DiyNatural.com/echinacea-benefits

Lemon Balm —

Lemon balm is an excellent plant to grow in your garden, as it has a wide range of medicinal uses. In addition to being a mosquito repellent, it is able to treat tons of conditions, such as sores, insect bites, fevers, headaches and depression. If you want to have this super herb in your house, keep in mind that it needs a fair amount of shade, and cutting it back may support regrowth.

Basil

Basil is not only popular in cooking, but also been widely used for medicinal purposes because of its several healthy properties. It contains antioxidants that even may help fight against cancer. It also can protect the body from premature aging, common skin issues and age-related problems. It's no need too much caution, basil may be grown in both sun and shade, the garden or a container, and prefers moist soil.

Sage

Sage is another great herb with medicinal properties. It is widely used to treat both internal and external conditions, including liver complaints, indigestion, anxiety, depression, skin infections and insect bites. Cuttings from grown sage plants are easier to grow, it requires yearly pruning and regular watering.

Sources: motherearthliving.com, eatlocalgrown.com, liveinthenow.com

Healing Foods

Note: This author has taken the unprecedented step of presenting the above information to you in an extremely convenient, readily available format so that you can come to one source to obtain the answer to address a host of nutritional deficiencies and self-treat a variety of minor injuries and illnesses. Nevertheless, because of potential legal ramifications from the powers that be, I am impelled to state that no information contained in this chapter should be utilized in lieu of prescribed treatment from your physician.

Next in line are the type of *healing* foods that should be purchased with practically every shopping trip to the market. But let's face it, most people, especially kids and teenagers are going to eat junk foods no matter what. That's why it's imperative to have these foods in your refrigerator and pantry at all times if at all possible. Literally thousands of recipes can be made from these nutritious items and the more they are served, the more your body will get used to and desire them. An introduction about each product below accompanies it, giving you a general idea of how beneficial they are to the health of your body.

Make no mistake about it, these important foods come chock-full of all the vitamins and minerals your body needs to grow and preserve bones, rejuvenate and condition the vast corridors of vessels: arteries, arterioles, capillaries, venules, and veins, as well as function to fight off the ravages of illnesses. They cleanse the blood, internal organs, and provide healing in every way, shape and form.

Apples

Because apples are high in pectin, a type of fiber that binds to cholesterol and heavy metals in the body, they help eliminate toxic build up, cleanse the intestines, and may possibly reduce the risk of many different types of cancers. Quercetin helps respiratory issues, like asthma, by clearing and relaxing the lungs allowing more oxygen in.

Food has certainly been the down-fall of man's health. With all the rubbish he stuffs into his delicate, yet adaptable organism, it is no wonder that there is so much unnatural disease rampant today. From the day he ate his first meal man has forever abused his system with the wrong types of food. He has not been rational in his eating habits, but has merely satisfied his banal desire for stimulating, refined and processed fare. The day will come, however, when he suddenly realizes that his food habits effect his physical as well as mental wellbeing. He will then realise that he had been satisfying his debased taste buds, rather than sustaining the body.

The wise, however, look toward nature for their answer; with patience and perseverance they have re-discovered the answer to man's dilemma. The answers although simple are extremely effective as they do not entail unnatural chemical compounds - it is the utilization of these wonderful gifts from nature which are so efficacious and free for all! There have been many natural curative formulae discovered throughout the centuries, which have proved themselves safe and yet effective. Natural resources have been used since the days before Christ viz: Sunshine, Water, Air—herbs and homebrews have been used for generations too by our ancestors. Honey is also a natural wonder, together with many other folk preparations which have been handed down through the ages. Amongst these **APPLE CIDER VINEGAR** has been widely used as a successful remedy for a number of ailments.

We find that, with the abuse of the body, inordinate amounts of waste matter have accumulated within the system. In the early stages these are not so apparent as the body is still vital enough to deal with this extra burden. However, if an attempt is not made to eradicate these toxic accumulations, the body has to deal with more and more pressure, resulting in aches and pains. Later in life these efforts to eliminate these encumberances result in influenza, bronchitis etc; and, if these healing efforts are suppressed by continued wrong living and drugs, the acute symptoms become chronic and insidious. Rheumatism, arthritis, cancer, heart ailments, high blood pressure etc, are all signs that the body has been neglected by the suppression of natural heating crisis. There are certain preparations, however, which assist the body in eliminating these toxic substances and this is where these natural curative methods have found a valuable place in the healing arts. To abstain from those foods and drinks which add to this unnecessary accumulation, is a great assistance to the body i.e. those refined and denatured food items such as bread, starch, white sugar, and their products; together with the unnecessary food items which cause excessive mucous and toxic waste in the system e.g. meat, eggs, dairy produce, legumes, cereals. However, one may now ask what should one eat if these are to be eliminated from the diet. Where one cannot completely abstain from these products, moderation is the key word in this instance, together with certain herbal and folk preparations which assist in the breakdown of the acids and mucous waste.

It is at this point that the benefits of APPLE CIDER VINEGAR will be discussed:

CIDER VINEGAR

"An apple a day keeps the doctor away" (the dentist too!) - is a cliché which should not be considered as just an obsolete "Old Wives Tale," as there is more than meets the eye in these axioms of yore. Apples are among the most health-giving fruits available as they contain a host of nutritious properties viz: Phosphorous, Cholerine, Potassium, Sodium, Magnesium, Calcium, Sulphur, Iron, Fluorine, Silicon, plus many trace elements .... and all of these are found in PURE APPLE CIDER VINEGAR.

WHAT DOES IT DO?

Amongst other things, cider vinegar is very effective in detoxicating various organs in the body together with the blood stream. Hence it is a purifier, as it has a means of breaking down fatty, mucous and phlegm deposits within the body. It therefore, promotes the health of the vital organs of the body e.g. kidneys, bladder, liver etc., by preventing an excessively alkaline urine. Cider vinegar also helps oxidate the blood which consequently prevents the blood from becoming too thick and gluey, which gives rise to a strained heart and blood vessels resulting in high blood pressure. Cider vinegar also promotes digestion, assimilation and elimination and it neutralizes any toxic substance taken into the body. There have been a number of instances where people who had taken a mixture of cider vinegar and water before a meal were unaffected by diarrhea, or digestive upsets, while their companions who ate the same meal were. Hence the cider vinegar seemed to neutralize the harmful substances in the food eaten.

POTASSIUM

Apple cider vinegar has a potent supply of potassium which has become so widely acclaimed in the helping of various complaints including: runny nose, excessive mucous formation, watery eyes, sinus and catarrhal troubles. Teeth decay and the splitting of finger nails are also signs of potassium deficiency which are remedied by taking cider vinegar. Potassium is essential for the normal growth of the body and for the replacement of worn-out tissues which depend upon the presence of this mineral. It is as important to the soft tissues, as calcium is to the bones and teeth and it also retards the hardening of the blood vessels.

As potassium is so important in the healthy growth of a plant, animal and human, a deficiency of this mineral will produce such tendencies as callous formations on the soles of the feet, or the failure to replace worn-out tissues as observed in the loss of hair.

Tests have proven that a soil deficient in this mineral-salt will produce anaemic and undersized plants, however, when potassium is introduced into the soil the plant becomes sturdier and increases in height. This is also the case with animals, where potassium which was fed to livestock, in the form of cider vinegar, improved their appearance and stamina. Humans too, can benefit with this increased potassium intake. Especially where children are slow developers and appear undersized. A few teaspoons of cider vinegar taken with water each morning will show tremendous results. The best way to introduce cider vinegar to the family, is to substitute it for the ordinary table vinegar and use it in the cooking. Potassium acts as a restraining influence upon those who are over-excitable and nervous. It draws fluid back into the cells, for when potassium is lacking the body cells shrink and their normal activity is restricted.

THE USES OF CIDER VINEGAR

A number of outstanding authorities have proven the therapeutic advantages of using cider vinegar for numerous complaints ranging from obesity and overweight to arthritis. Besides the therapeutic benefits derived from taking cider vinegar therapy, as outlined in this book, it can also be used for a number of other purposes e.g. salad dressing, pickling, a flavour in cooking etc. It also makes a very refreshing drink, hot or cold, with or without honey - this should take the place of normal tea and coffee which are so habit-forming and unnecessary commodities.

Try using cider vinegar where lemon juice is required e.g. in making mayonnaise, or just sprinkle some on a salad before serving; sprinkle on pawpaw for a refreshing breakfast, or just use on potato chips!

EFFECTS OF CIDER VINEGAR ON THE BLOOD

When the blood is deficient in some minerals or biochemic salt, ill-health is the outcome e.g. boils break out, suppurating blisters become apparent, pimples appear on the face etc. It has been found however, that cider vinegar helps with the cleansing as well as the clotting of the blood. Oxidation of the blood is very important and cider vinegar is again an effective treatment for this. Besides introducing the important minerals into the blood stream, as mentioned above, cider vinegar also helps in the clotting of blood. This is of tremendous help to those people who are commonly termed 'bleeders', as they live their lives in fear of cutting themselves due to the bloods inability to clot, and it will also enhance the healing process.

AILMENTS
ARTHRITIS:

Use the cider vinegar and honey treatment for arthritis and also apply cider vinegar externally to painful joints. This entails drinking a glass of water with two teaspoons of cider vinegar and two teaspoons of honey three times a day. Local treatment can also be given by soaking the arthritic hand, or foot in a strong, comfortably hot solution of cider vinegar for ten minutes, two or three times a day - (a quarter of a cup of cider vinegar to one and a half cups of water). Arthritic knees can be attended to by making a poultice - soak the cloth in a mixture of cider vinegar and water, (as per above mixture) wring out and wrap it around the joint, then secure with a dry cloth to retain heat. When the wet cloth cools, it should be wrung out in the hot solution and applied afresh. Repeat several times, twice daily.

ASTHMA:

One tablespoonful of cider vinegar added to a glass of water should be taken in sips for half an hour. After a further half an hour has elapsed the treatment should be repeated. The wheezing should lessen in intensity quite considerably. However, should wheezing still persist a second glass of the same mixture should be taken. Deep breathing exercises are also a beneficial treatment.

BLOOD LOSS:

It has been discussed above how cider vinegar helps in preventing blood losses. In any circumstances where the flow of blood is too free and is too persistent, such as when a person has a nose bleed without any apparent reason, then two teaspoons of cider vinegar in a glass of water, three times a day will aid in restoring the natural clotting properties of the blood.

COLITIS:

The cider vinegar and honey treatment has been used effectively in the treatment for colitis. Take the normal dosage of two teaspoons cider vinegar and honey with water, three times a day. An enema of a teaspoonful or more of molasses is also very helpful.

COUGHS:

There are many types of coughs for various reasons, and these should be treated with reference to their nature and intensity. However, the cider vinegar and honey treatment will prove an efficacious treatment in this respect. Two teaspoons of cider vinegar and two of honey mixed with a glassful of water should be taken before meals, or when the irritation occurs. In the evening it would be an idea to have this mixture by your bed so that it can be sipped during the evening if an attack presents itself.

DIARRHEA:

It has been mentioned above how cider vinegar helps with the digestion, assimilation and elimination of food, and that it is an antiseptic to the intestines and the whole of the digestive tract. Due to it's healing properties, diarrhea can be controlled in a very short time, (that is unless some serious physical disorder is apparent). The treatment being, one teaspoonful of cider vinegar in a glass of water should be taken before and inbetween meals i.e. approximately six glasses during the course of the day. It should be noted, however, that diarrhoea is a natural attempt on the part of the body to eliminate some poison which is irritating the digestive tract, on no account should any drugs be taken to suppress these healing symptoms - on the other hand the cider vinegar will lessen the intensity, but will allow the natural course of elimination to take place.

DIZZINESS:

Two teaspoons of apple cider vinegar together with two teaspoons of honey in a glass of hot or cold water three times a day should help this annoying occurrence quite considerably. However, one should never expect instant results, as nature works slowly, yet very effectively. You will notice a lessened intensity while you progress.

EAR DISCHARGE:

The treatment for this complaint, which usually occurs during childhood is: one teaspoonful of cider vinegar in a glass of water to be taken mid morning and mid afternoon. The discharge should shortly disappear.

ECZEMA:

Take the usual dosage of cider vinegar and honey in a glassful of water three times a day, with meals. An application of well diluted cider vinegar can also be applied to the skin several times daily i.e. one teaspoonful to half a cup of water. Under no circumstances should salt be taken, as this aggravates the eczema condition considerably. There is usually a potassium deficiency in those people suffering from eczema.

EYES (TIRED AND SORE):

The cider vinegar therapy together with honey is the essential ingredients here. Two teaspoons of each taken in a glassful of water, three times a day. This mixture retards the onset of tired and sore eyes which are usually apparent in later life, as it supplies them with those vital elements essential to their health and functioning.

FATIGUE:

Chronic fatigue is a warning that the body needs some attention. Most people suffering from chronic fatigue do not have enough good, sound sleep. Either they go to bed too late, or they are one of those people who just need more sleep than most. It is better to get as many hours in bed before midnight as possible. To remedy a poor quality sleep, honey is highly recommended, as it acts as a sedative to the body. Twenty minutes after the honey has been taken into the mouth it has been digested and absorbed into the body. This is because it is a predigested sugar, which has been digested in the stomach of the honey bee, and therefore requires no effort on the part of the human stomach for digestion. Keep the following mixture by your bedside to be taken as indicated: three teaspoons of honey to a cup of apple cider vinegar.

Take two teaspoons of the mixture before retiring. This should induce sound sleep within an hour, if however, you have been unable to sleep within this period repeat the dosage.

FOOD POISONING:

As mentioned earlier there have been many cases where people who were in the habit of taking cider vinegar regularly never suffer any side effects from food poisoning. The cider vinegar has an antiseptic quality which seems to render noxious food harmless.

HAIR LOSS:

The falling out of hair is primarily due to a tissue salt deficiency, thus cider vinegar with its 'wonder products' will re-establish a natural balance, and supply the deficiencies where needed. Therefore, by taking the cider vinegar treatment the hair will maintain its natural growth. It will cease to fall out and grow more rapidly and thickly. This will take approximately two months, so perseverence is needed. The dosage is one teaspoonful of cider vinegar to a glass of water to be taken with or between meals. Cider vinegar can also be used externally for the treatment of dandruff, see under heading of External Treatments.

HAYFEVER:

This ailment is marked by watery eyes, sneezing and running nose, in other words there is an excess of fluid which the body is drastically trying to offload. For an effective relief, honey and cider vinegar should be utilized which will bring excellent results. A tablespoonful of honey should be taken after each meal for approximately a fortnight before the onset of the hay-fever season. The ordinary dosage of cider vinegar and honey should then be taken viz: two teaspoons of cider vinegar and two of honey in a glass of water, three times a day. This dosage should be maintained during the entire hay-fever season.

HEADACHES:

There are several types of headache, caused by various reasons. Some are associated with organic disorders, such as kidney troubles, others are known as psychogenic, or tension headaches. Then we have the most annoying of all; the migraine headache. Many people have had relief from headaches by the use of honey. Two teaspoons taken at each meal may well prevent an attack. Another effective means is to take apple cider vinegar. Equal parts of cider vinegar and water should be placed in a small basin on the stove, allowing it to boil slowly. When the fumes begin to rise from the basin lean your head over it until the fumes are comfortably strong. Inhale for approximately 50 to 80 breaths. Generally this alleviates the headache considerably, if not entirely.

HEARING:

(Impaired) The treatment of impaired hearing has had excellent results on the apple cider vinegar therapy. Take the normal dosage three times daily and notice the improvement.

HEARTBURN:

This usually occurs after eating, sometimes up to two hours later. This very unpleasant feeling can be alleviated by taking the usual dosage of cider vinegar and water before meals.

HEMORRHAGES:

As previously pointed out cider vinegar helps the blood to clot more easily. When a person who regularly drinks cider vinegar cuts himself, the wound will dry up almost instantaneously, as there will be no profuse bleeding. If, however, wounds do not heal quickly, the following procedure should be undertaken; two teaspoons of cider vinegar taken in half or a whole glass of water at mealtimes as well as in between, therefore six glasses in all are imbibed. For extra efficiency a very weak solution of cider vinegar with water can be applied to the sore, wound or cut.

Poultices of cider vinegar (see instructions under the heading Arthritis) can be applied to a stubborn open wound.

HICCOUGHS (HICCUPS):

These have been known to be eradicated by drinking a teaspoon of cider vinegar neat! Alternatively cider vinegar with water can be taken before mealtimes to prevent this occurrence.

HIGH BLOOD PRESSURE:

There are a number of reasons why a person suffers from this common yet serious condition. As mentioned earlier, health will be maintained only if one is prepared to adjust his living and eating habits. Cider vinegar is not the cure-all of man's suffering, it is only one of the many means towards a healthier and happier life. In the case of High Blood Pressure, one's eating habits must be taken stock of to ensure a speedy and effective recovery. Emphasis is on the natural, organically grown foods which are given to us in the form of fresh fruits, vegetables and honey - rather than the high protein foods which include eggs, meat, milk, cheese, nuts, beans etc. A balance must be maintained between the proteins and carbohydrates and one should definitely not over indulge on these protein and starchy foods. Wheat products should also be eliminated completely, together with salt which is very detrimental to the health, especially for those suffering from high blood pressure. The following dosage should be taken daily: two teaspoons of apple cider vinegar and honey in a glass of water - up to three to four times a day.

INSOMNIA:

There are also a number of causes as to why people suffer from insomnia; however, there have been excellent results with the cider vinegar and honey treatment as follows: two teaspoons of cider vinegar and two of honey in a glass of water to be taken before retiring. It would also be beneficial to have a glass of this mixture by the bedside to sip if needed. Under no circumstances should drugs be resorted to, as these are both harmful and habit-forming. Under severe cases, a naturopath or homeopath should be consulted. If has been found that the prime cause of insomnia is due to a deficiency of phosphate of potash and phosphate of iron; this combination can be found in the biochemic salt known as kali phos, which can be obtained from your local health shop.

KIDNEYS AND BLADDER:

Due to the eliminative nature of cider vinegar, the kidneys and bladder can benefit tremendously by a 'flushing' which they receive when the following cider vinegar therapy is undertaken: two teaspoons of cider vinegar in a glass of water six times a day. It would be beneficial to drink a couple of glasses of water in the morning, taking one teaspoonful of cider vinegar in each drink. Comfrey tea, first thing in the morning with a teaspoon of cider vinegar will also create a sufficient cleansing action. Inflammation of the kidneys, called pyelitis, in which pus cells are present in the urine, will generally clear up with the above-mentioned treatment.

MENSTRUATION:

Chronic pains and profuse menstruation has afflicted women for centuries. The cider vinegar therapy certainly regulates and normalizes profuse bleeding. The dosage should be as normal, i.e. two teaspoons of cider vinegar in a glassful of water three times a day. The diet should also be taken into consideration, as a high animal protein diet together with wheat products will cause considerable pain when the periods begin. In other words moderation should be used if one is partaking of these foods. However, meat, poultry, fish and wheat should be completely eliminated from the diet, together with the other unnatural foods of which man is so prone. A noticeable improvement will be experienced when the diet is kept to the fresh raw fruits and fresh salads, together with the apple cider vinegar therapy. Also plenty of water should be taken while menstruating, as this helps in a speedy elimination.

MUCOUS DISCHARGES:

Postnasal drips and watery eyes are also due to a faulty diet, here again this should be thoroughly investigated, as the body is eliminating excessive mucous caused by the wrong types of food. This is often caused by a lack of potassium in the diet too, hence the cider vinegar therapy will help considerably. The usual dosage as prescribed above should be taken three times a day before meals. Wheat should be eliminated from the diet completely and rye and corn products should be substituted, if required.

NAIL PROBLEMS:

Brittle, cracking, fragile and thin nails are a sign of some deficiency and faulty metabolism in the body. Cider vinegar has been known to remedy this particular complaint, with the results of healthy, strong nails. Also any white spots which were present on the nails previously will be eliminated. Dosage being: two teaspoons in a glassful of water three times a day.

NERVOUSNESS:

There have been cases where nervousness has been remedied with the cider vinegar and honey treatment. In this instance a glassful of water mixed with two teaspoons of each, i.e. cider vinegar and honey to be taken three times a day. Refined flour and sugar products should be completely eliminated from the diet, together with wheat products. One should also cut down on the starch and high protein foods as much as possible and eat plenty of fresh salads and fruit.

NOSE BLEED:

As an excessive nose bleed is caused by the blood being unable to clot as it should normally, the cider vinegar treatment will prove efficacious in this respect i.e. two teaspoons of cider vinegar in a glassful of water three times daily.

NOSE - STUFFY:

In this respect the cider vinegar can be used as an inhalant. Use as per method described under the heading Headaches. The nasal passages will shortly clear after having inhaled the vapour. This treatment is very effective in removing the congestion in the sinuses, together with any inflammation which may result from this excessive accumulation of mucous.

OBESITY:

There are a number of reasons why a person is assailed with excessive fat deposits. This is apparent in both sexes and cannot, from professional data, be attributed to any one major factor. Obesity, often eventuates from the excessive intake of alcohol, thereby causing water retention in the tissues. This is often apparent by the 'swollen' appearance of the face. There are also certain drugs which are apt to cause obesity and thus the body increases in weight. Overeating, insufficient oxidation of the blood, insufficient exercise, lack of fresh air etc, are also attributed to this ailment. However, Cyril Scott mentions in his booklet on cider vinegar that the prime cause of obesity is the insufficient oxidation of the blood, he goes on to say, "Now the safe and salubrious treatment, proved over years of trial, is to be found in nothing more complicated than cider vinegar - the reason being, as already implied, that the ailment is conductive to the proper oxidation of the blood." Two teaspoons of cider vinegar should be taken in a glassful of water on rising in the morning. To obtain the best results possible this should be taken before each meal and during the day over a period of some time. Natural methods always take longer to work, as the body has to adapt itself, especially the skin in this instance, as if too much weight is lost in a short period of time, then it will hang and look unsightly. The drink should be sipped during the course of the meal which will also prevent overeating and it will promote digestion. According to some authorities, the average weight reduction is 1.5 lbs. a week. This all depends upon whether the diet has been adjusted. Salt should be discontinued immediately as this harmful commodity retains water - herbal beverages such as comfrey should take the place of tea and coffee. Wholesome, nutritious and moderation is the key to weight loss, together with deep breathing and physical exercise.

SHINGLES:

Cider vinegar relieves the pain arising from shingles if applied, undiluted, six times daily to the area of distress. It also promotes the healing. Take internally as well as prescribed above.

SORE THROAT:

To treat this, one should gargle with apple cider vinegar. One teaspoonful of vinegar in a glass of water is the dosage to be used. A mouthful of this solution is gargled every hour, and the second mouthful after gargling should be swollowed. This is to be repeated every hour until the condition of the throat is improved.

TEETH:

Due to cider vinegar improving the calcium metabolism of the body, it is excellent for improving the condition of the teeth. Tartar deposits can also be eradicated by using the cider vinegar as a mouthwash and by brushing your teeth with it to enhance the whiteness. For the mouthwash, one teaspoonful of cider vinegar should be added to a glassful of water - repeat this procedure each night until the required results are achieved. This habit, together with the drinking of cider vinegar will prevent tooth decay quite considerably. The mouthwash can also be used for sore gums, or ulcerated gums - be sure that the solution is not too strong in this case, as it will slightly sting an open sore.

VARICOSE VEINS:

Apply undiluted cider vinegar to the area where the veins are affected. This should be undertaken in the morning and evening. Massage well - always directed towards the heart, e.g. as in the case of the legs, start from the ankles and move in upward strokes towards the thigh. Cider vinegar and honey should also be taken three times a day, i.e. two teaspoons of cider vinegar and two of honey mixed with a glassful of water.

WEIGHT GAIN:

As cider vinegar supplies those organs of the body which are deficient in some mineral and normalizes the functioning of these organs, those who are underweight will find that cider vinegar will help in normalizing their weight. In this instance the following dosage should be adhered to: two teaspoons of cider vinegar and two of honey in a glass of water three times a day.

WEIGHT LOSS:

(Also see Obesity) Cider vinegar will gradually decrease the weight of the body, as it tends to make the body burn up the fat instead of storing it. Some people have had results by just taking the cider vinegar without adjusting their eating habits. However, it is recommended that one should concentrate on the LIVE FOODS, rather than continue to live on the devitalized diet which is so prevalent today. The cider vinegar method, as mentioned under Obesity should be utilized three times daily.

EXTERNAL APPLICATIONS

The skin is a very important part of the body, as it is the major organ of elimination. Besides being an effective eliminator the skin also absorbs substances into the body. In view of this fact it is very important to understand that we should be very careful with what we place on the skin. Unnatural substances such as cosmetics, which contain chemicals are very detrimental to the skin health. This is also true for the commercial soap we use for washing the body. The skin needs an acid mantle to maintain its lustre and glow - however, due to the extreme alkalinity of soap reacting on the skin, this causes a number of disorders. Soap also contains animal fats and hormones, synthetic perfumes and preservatives; therefore, it should not be used to cleanse the body.

However, cider vinegar is an effective method of cleansing the body. A hand bath should be preceded as follows. to half a glass of warm water should be added one teaspoonful of apple cider vinegar. Cup the palm of the hand and pour in approximately a palmful of the mixture. First apply to the arms and shoulders, rubbing the solution into the skin briskly. The legs and feet can be done in the same manner, together with the body. A brisk rubbing action should be used to massage the cider vinegar solution into the skin. You will soon find that the solution has been completely absorbed by the skin, therefore, no towelling down is needed.

FOR A BATH:

Instead of using soap, add a half pint of apple cider vinegar to the water and remain submerged in the water for at least fifteen minutes so that the skin surface of the body may have a chance to absorb some of the acid water. This is extremely important for those people who have an alkaline skin; this condition will be indicated by those people who continually suffer from skin irritation, and they are forever scratching their skin.

ITCHY SCALP:

Take one teaspoonful of apple cider vinegar mixed with a glassful of water - dip your comb into the solution and comb the hair thoroughly until saturated. This should be performed fifteen minutes or so before actually washing the hair. This treatment also helps with the elimination of dandruff.

Source: http://www.tbyil.com/acv.htm

**Avocados**. We rarely think of avocados as a cleansing food. However, these nutritional powerhouses lower cholesterol and dilate blood vessels while blocking artery-destroying toxicity. Avocados contain a nutrient, called glutathione, which blocks at least thirty different carcinogens while helping the liver detoxify synthetic chemicals.

**Beets**. Time to whip up some delicious borscht soup since its main ingredient, beets, contain a unique mixture of natural plant compounds that make them superb blood purifiers and liver cleansers.

**Blueberries**. Truly one of the most powerful healing foods. Blueberries contain natural aspirin that helps lessen the tissue-damaging effects of chronic inflammation, while lessening pain. Blueberries also act as antibiotics by blocking bacteria in the urinary tract, thereby helping to prevent infections. Blueberries have antiviral properties and help to block toxins from crossing the blood-brain barrier to gain access to the delicate brain.

**Cabbage**. Cabbage contains numerous anticancer and antioxidant compounds and helps the liver break down excess hormones. Cabbage also cleanses the digestive tract and neutralizes some of the damaging compounds found in cigarette smoke (and second-hand smoke). It also strengthens the liver's ability to detoxify.

Celery and Celery Seeds. Celery and celery seeds are excellent blood cleansers and contain many different anti-cancer compounds that help detoxify cancer cells in the body. Celery seeds contain over twenty anti-inflammatory substances. Celery is particularly good for detoxifying substances found in cigarette smoke.

Cranberries. Cleanse your body from harmful bacteria and viruses that may be lingering in your urinary tract with cranberries since they contain antibiotic and antiviral substances.

Flaxseeds and Flaxseed Oil. Loaded with essential fatty acids, particularly the Omega-3s, flaxseeds and flaxseed oil are essential for many cleansing functions throughout the body.

Garlic. Eat garlic to cleanse harmful bacteria, intestinal parasites and viruses from your body, especially from the blood and intestines. Garlic also helps cleanse build-up from the arteries and has anti-cancer and antioxidant properties that help detoxify the body of harmful substances. Additionally, garlic assists with cleansing the respiratory tract by expelling mucous build-up in the lungs and sinuses. For the health benefits, choose only fresh garlic, not garlic powder, which has virtually none of the above properties.

Grapefruit. Add a ruby red grapefruit to your breakfast to benefit from pectin fiber that binds to cholesterol, thereby cleansing the blood. Pectin also

binds to heavy metals and helps escort them out of the body. It also has antiviral compounds that cleanse harmful viruses out of the body. Grapefruit is an excellent intestinal and liver detoxifier.

Kale. Steam some kale to benefit from its powerful anti-cancer and antioxidant compounds that help cleanse the body of harmful substances. It is also high in fiber, which helps cleanse the intestinal tract. Like cabbage, kale helps neutralize compounds found in cigarette smoke and strengthens liver cleansing.

Legumes. Add a handful of cooked beans to your next meal. They are loaded with fiber that helps lower cholesterol, cleanses the intestines, and regulates blood sugar levels. Legumes also help protect the body against cancer.

Lemons. Excellent liver detoxifiers, lemons contain high amounts of vitamin C, a vitamin needed by the body to make an important substance called glutathione. Glutathione helps the liver detoxify harmful chemicals. Add a squeeze of fresh lemon juice (not the bottled variety) to pure water to support your cleansing efforts on a daily basis. See Lemons, Ginger, Papaya, Coconut oil, and Nuts below for more details.

Seaweed. Seaweed could be the most underrated vegetable in the western world. Studies at McGill University in Montreal showed that seaweed binds to radioactive waste

in the body. Seaweed also binds to heavy metals to help eliminate them from the body. In addition, seaweed is a powerhouse of minerals and trace minerals.

Watercress. If you haven't tried watercress, add this delicious green to your next sandwich. Watercress increases detoxification enzymes and acts on cancer cells in the body. In a study at the Norwich Food Research Centre in the United Kingdom, smokers who were given 170 grams of watercress per day eliminated higher than average amounts of carcinogens in their urine, thereby eliminating them from their body.

Eating a variety of fresh fruits and vegetables assists with detoxifying harmful substances from your body. Who knew cleansing could taste so good?

Arthor's note: Organic foods are available Online at - www.More.sh/Organic-Healthfood

Adapted with permission from: The 4-Week Ultimate Body Detox Plan by Michelle Schoffro Cook (John Wiley & Sons, 2006). Copyright Michelle Schoffro Cook.

Michelle Schoffro Cook, RNCP, ROP, DAc, DNM, is a best-selling and six-time book author and doctor of natural medicine, whose works include: The Life Force Diet, The Ultimate pH Solution, *and* The 4-Week Ultimate Body Detox Plan. *Learn more at:* www.TheLifeForceDiet.com.

More on Diet & Nutrition (264 articles available) **More from Michelle Schoffro Cook** (38 articles available)

Lemons, Ginger, Papaya, Coconut oil, and Nuts

Because they are so common, found practically anywhere in the world, the following products are largely ignored regarding the exceptional benefits ascribed to them. Their potency are actually played down by the powers that be. Therefore, I am including detailed information about each of them so that you will know the inherent power contained within the walls of these powerhouses and be better able to make an informed decision about taking responsibility for your own health.

Let's start with the common lemon that can be found in practically any and all types of markets, both small and large. I believe that once people begin to understand how truly powerful just these products are, there will probably be a run on them at every market.

LEMONS: Medicine cabinet within a fruit

Recent research by modern scientists has confirmed what the Ancient Egyptians believed thousands of years ago, that eating lemons and drinking the juice, was an effective protection against a variety of poisons.

The legalized drug trade, known as the pharmaceutical industry, makes a concerted effort via large-scale commercial media and multimillion dollar advertising to maximize the news about their toxic drugs and severely minimize the supreme power of fruits like lemons. But, together, let's look at the truth of what they accomplish:

1. antibacterial,

2. antiviral,

3. immune-boosting powers,

4. digestive aid,

5. liver cleanser,

6. weight loss

7. Repel mosquitoes

The Problem: Millions of people around the nation have been duped into believing that the Fall-Winter period is the so-called Flu season, and have already resolved in their collective mind that Flu shots and antibiotics they obtain from the doctor takes care of everything.

How absurd! Unfortunately, nearly all patients deeply believe the advice of their allopathic (the term for an MD) doctors, who only seek to solve your problem with chemicals... newer and newer chemicals the pharmaceutical industry continuously bombard them with. If patients clearly understood the lucrative monetary kickbacks these doctors receive, they wouldn't be so quick to rush to them for something so simple as a cold. Something extremely important to understand is that your regular family physician gets paid to do two things:

1. Find out what your *symptom* is (diagnose),

2. Prescribe the pharmaceutical chemical to ease **ONLY** the symptom.

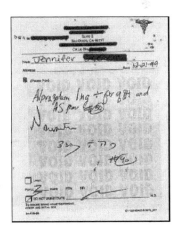

When you receive that small slip of paper with their office contact information printed on it, and some undecipherable scribbling, that lets the pharmacist know to send that particular doctor a percentage of the money they receive after you pay $385,000.00 for your prescription. Yes! That's an exaggeration, but we all know that prescriptions are expensive. In essence, the doctor gets paid in three ways:

1. From the co-pay your insurance requests, unless you pay extra to avoid a co-payment.

2. Remuneration from your insurance company,

3. A percentage of the proceeds from the sale of a prescription. (Ahhh! Now you know why they're so quick to prescribe a useless antibiotic to you for a simple cold or Flu, right?)

Oh! And don't forget the kickbacks they also receive from the pharmaceutical industry for using you as a guinea pig to test the latest drug.

If you have a cold or Flu, one of the silliest things a person can do is go to his/her doctor for antibiotics. Antibiotics are a group of medicines that are used to treat infections caused by **bacteria** and certain parasites. They **DO NOT** work against infections that are caused by **viruses** - for example, the common cold or flu. But, trying to tell that to the mass public is like trying to tell a 3-year-old child that there is no such thing as ghosts. So, since doctors are not paid to take the time to *advise* you on the root of your malady, and do not know which foods to teach you to eat for complete health and rejuvenation, they resort to killing you softly.

Which brings us to the validity of this book. It gives you the unhindered, factual information you need to make an informed choice about your body, not depend 100% on the sickness industry, and enjoy making you a person of indomitable health. So, this author previously wrote a short article mostly how lemons help the skin. But now, let's take a look at how truly **SUPER** powerful this fruit really is.

Lemons contain many substances—notably citric acid, calcium, magnesium, vitamin C, bioflavonoids, pectin, and limonene—that promote immunity and fight infection. You won't find even one pharmaceutical drug that will provide effective benefits like that. Whether you use them in the form of juice, teas, drinks, dressing, poultices or in the bath, take advantage of lemons' natural healing power. The above are well-known health facts about lemons. But if you don't know the additional benefits of this small yellow fruit it will surely amaze you.

Lemon is well known for its medicinal power and is used in many different ways. As per the results reported in a study by the Annals of the Rheumatic Diseases, lemon provides protection against inflammatory polyarthritis and arthritis.

Research has shown that lemon balm has a calming effect and therefore may be able to help remove fatigue, exhaustion, dizziness, nervousness, and tension. It is also believed that inhaling lemon oil helps in increasing concentration and alertness, promote sleep, improve appetite, reduce stress and anxiety, and ease pain and discomfort from indigestion (including gas and bloating, as well as colic). The juice of a lemon includes its use as a treatment of throat infections, indigestion, constipation, dental problems, and fever; internal bleeding, rheumatism, burns, obesity, respiratory disorders, cholera and high blood pressure, while it also benefits hair and skin care. Lemons has been known for its therapeutic property since generations past.

Below is a GOLDMINE of the true power and health benefits of lemons:

CANKER SORE - The proven antibacterial and antiviral properties of lemons can accelerate the healing process in the case of cankers. Mix the juice of freshly squeezed lemon into a glass of lukewarm water and rinse your mouth with this solution; do this three times a day. There may be a burning sensation when the lemon juice comes into contact with the canker, however, the more frequently you use it, the less burning there will be.

CHILLS & FEVER - This may be due to a variety of causes, but the lemon is always a helpful remedy. Here is a method that can ease symptoms: add the freshly-squeezed juice of 1 whole lemon to a cup (8 oz) of tepid (lukewarm) water drink all of it down at once. Then, repeat about every 2 hours until the fever or chill subsides. If the taste is just too bitter for you, there's two ways to make it more enjoyable. Hold your breathe while drinking it down, or add some honey to taste.

COLDS - Now, as soon as you feel the slightest symptom of a cold coming on—a runny nose or sore throat—**DON'T WAIT!** Immediately get a lemon and follow the procedure above to give your body as much immune-boosting vitamin C as you can so that the virus is eliminated **BEFORE** it gets a chance to take hold. The healing power of lemons works both internally, by supplying urgently required vitamin C to your defense cells, and externally, through the application of its antiviral properties to the virus on the mucous membranes in the nose and throat.

So at the first indication of a cold, drink the freshly squeezed juice of 1 lemon in a glass of lukewarm water every 2 hours.

SORE THROAT - If you have a sore throat, add the juice of 1 lemon and 1 teaspoon (5ml) of sea salt to 1 cup (250ml) lukewarm water. Gargle three times a day for 1 minute to diminish the burning sensation. If it's a case of tonsillitis, gargle every 2 hours for at least 30 seconds with the freshly squeezed juice of 1 lemon. Tilt the head back to allow the antibacterial and antiviral properties of the juice to flow into the back of the throat. You can swallow the juice when you have finished gargling thereby benefiting from an immune-boosting vitamin C shot.

CORNS & CALLUSES - Lemon poultices applied overnight are a good home remedy for corns and calluses. Place a slice of lemon approx 5 mm thick on to the corn, bandage and fasten. Dabbing the affected area with lemon essential oil also helps accelerate the healing process. Take care to only use the undiluted oil on the callused area using a cotton ball or Q- tip, as it is too strong for un-callused skin.

ECZEMA - If you suffer from skin infection such as eczema, a lemon wrap may offer relief. Add 8 drops of lemon essential oil to 1 cup (250ml) lukewarm water and 1 tablespoon (15ml) of liquid honey. Honey also has anti-inflammatory effect and strengthens the healing power of lemon.

Soak a linen cloth in the liquid, squeeze out the excess, and gently place the cloth on the affected area for 15 minutes, 2 to 3 times a day. Not only will this ease the infection, it will counter the overwhelming urge to scratch.

FATIGUE - Long distance walkers, world travelers, and explorers look upon the lemon as a Godsend. When fatigue sets in, they might suck lemon juice by piercing the top of the fruit with a straw, giving themselves a quick-acting medicine and a lovely refreshment.

Explorers also use lemon for protection against many infections of the tropics. A small amount of lemon juice will quench thirst more effectively than many times the amount of water. Experienced travelers declare that when they add lemon juice to ordinary drinking water, in various localities, it acts as an antiseptic and prevents illness due to allergy to different water supplies.

Lemon oil also seems to be able to stimulate brain activity so whenever you feel tired for no reason or are finding it hard to focus or concentrate, add 4 drops of lemon oil to a water-filled aromatherapy lamp. Alternatively, drink a glass of lemon water every few hours.

BREATH FRESHENER - Lemons can help freshen breath that has gone sour after consuming certain spices, alcohol, cigarettes, or that is caused by insufficient salivation. To keep breath fresh, thoroughly rinse your mouth several times a day with the freshly squeezed juice of 1 lemon in a glass of lukewarm water. Chewing on a lemon slice after every meal will also help.

HIGH BLOOD PRESSURE - Garlic and onions have been shown to be effective in the fight against hypertension (high blood pressure), and they combine well with the healing power of lemon. Add 3 crushed garlic cloves and 1 chopped onion to 1 quart or cold skimmed or low fat milk or soy milk. Slowly bring to the boil and let it stand for 5 minutes. Pour through a sieve and chill. Add the freshly squeezed juice of 3 lemons and sip throughout the day.

And if you suffer from high cholesterol, don't forget that the pectin power in lemons along with its other metabolism and circulation boosting nutrients can help lower cholesterol.

BEE STING - Ever get stung by a bee? If the stinger is still in the skin, take it out with a pair of tweezers. Massage 1 to 2 drops of lemon oil, mixed with 1 teaspoon of honey, into the skin around the bite.

MOSQUITO REPELLENT To repel insects, add 20 drops of lemon oil to 1 cup (250ml) of water and spray into the air. It smells great and repels insects at the same time. Another home remedy is to place a cotton ball soaked in lemon oil in your bedroom. If you are sitting outside in the evening, apply lemon scent to skin areas not covered in clothing. Or, add 10 drops of lemon oil to 1 ½ oz of sunflower oil and rub into the skin.

RHEUMATISM - Even though it tastes bitter, lemon juice has a powerful alkaline effect in the body and is therefore a natural agent against excess acid, which is in part responsible for rheumatism. Drink the freshly squeezed juice of 1 lemon in a glass of lukewarm water 3 times a day and if you experience severe pain add the juice of 2 lemons 3 times a day.

PAIN-RELIEVER - Lemon oil has pain-relieving qualities, so to inhibit inflammation and ease pain, massage the affected area daily with several drops of lemon oil mixed with 1 tablespoon (15ml) jojoba oil.

VARICOSE VEINS - Lemon oil has vessel-strengthening properties that can help fight varicose and spider veins. For spider veins, take 2 to 3 drops of lemon oil every day and mix in a small bowl with jojoba, avocado or almond oil and massage the affected area.

For varicose veins, add 6 drops of lemon oil to 1 ½ oz (50 ml) wheat germ oil, and 2 drops each of cypress and juniper oil. Use this mixture daily for a gentle massage of the legs from bottom to top, in the direction of the heart. For a vein and vessel-rejuvenating bath add 8 drops of lemon oil to a warm bath. Also add 4 drops of cypress oil blended with 1 tablespoon (15ml) of honey. Soak in the bath for 15 minutes and when you come out, pat your skin dry – don't rub it.

KIDNEY STONES - Lemon juice, especially, has several health benefits associated with it. It is well known as a useful treatment for kidney stones, reducing strokes and lowering body temperature. As a refreshing drink, lemonade helps you to stay calm and cool.

HAIR CARE - Lemon juice has proven itself in the treatment of hair care on a wide scale. Lemon juice applied to the scalp can treat problems like dandruff, hair loss and other problems related to the hair and scalp. If you apply lemon juice directly on the hair, it can give your hair a natural shine.

The health benefits of lemons are due to its many nourishing elements like vitamin C, vitamin B, phosphorous, proteins, and carbohydrates. Lemon is a fruit that contains flavonoids, which are composites that contain antioxidant and cancer fighting properties. It helps to prevent diabetes, constipation, high blood pressure, fever, indigestion and many other problems, as well as improving the skin, hair, and teeth. Studies conducted at the American Urological Association highlight the fact that lemonade or lemon juice can eliminate the occurrence of kidney stones by forming urinary citrate, which prevents the formation of crystals.

People use lemons to make lemonade by mixing lemon juice and water. Many people also use lemon as a washing agent, because of its ability to remove stains. The scent of lemon can also repel mosquitoes, while drinking lemon juice with olive oil helps to get rid of gall stones.

SKIN CARE - Lemon juice, being a natural antiseptic medicine, can also cure problems related to the skin. Lemon juice can be applied to reduce the pain of sun burn, and it helps to ease the pain from bee stings as well. Lemon juice can be applied on the skin for the treatment of acne and eczema. It acts as an anti-aging remedy and can remove wrinkles and blackheads. Drinking lemon juice mixed with water and honey brings a healthy glow to the skin, and if you thoroughly search the cosmetic market, you will find some soaps containing lemon juice, but they aren't too easy to find!

BURNS - Application of lemon juice on the site of old burns can help fade the scars, and since lemon is a cooling agent, it reduces the burning sensation on the skin when you currently have an irritating burn.

TOOTHACHE - Lemon juice is also frequently used in dental care. If fresh lemon juice is applied on the area of a toothache, it can assist in getting rid of the pain. Massaging lemon juice on the gums can stop gum bleeding, while eliminating the bad odors that can come from various gum diseases and conditions.

INTERNAL BLEEDING - Lemon has antiseptic and coagulant properties, so it can stop internal bleeding. You can apply lemon juice to a small cotton ball and place it inside your nose to stop nose bleeds.

WEIGHT LOSS - If a person drinks lemon juice mixed with lukewarm water and honey, it can help reduce body weight.

RESPIRATORY DISORDERS - Lemon juice assists in relieving respiratory problems and breathing problems, such as its ability to soothe a person suffering from an asthma attack. Lemon, as a rich rich source of vitamin C, helps in dealing with more long-term respiratory disorders.

CHOLERA - Diseases like cholera and malaria can be treated with lemon juice, because it acts as a blood purifier.

FOOT RELAXATION - Lemon is an aromatic and antiseptic agent and is useful in foot relaxation. Add some lemon juice to warm water and dip your feet in the mixture for instant relief and muscle relaxation.

RHEUMATISM - Lemon is also a diuretic and can treat rheumatism and arthritis. It helps to flush out bacteria and toxins from the body.

CORNS - Lemon juice can dissolve lumps on the skin, so it can be applied at the places where the skin has hardened up, like the soles of feet and the palms of your hands. Drinking lemon juice with water can help patients reduce gall stones for the same reasons.

THROAT INFECTIONS - Lemon is an excellent fruit that fights against problems related to throat infections, due to its well-known antibacterial properties.

HIGH BLOOD PRESSURE - Drinking lemon juice is helpful for people suffering from heart problems, because it contains potassium. It controls high blood pressure, dizziness, and nausea, because it provides a calming sensation to both the mind and body. It is commonly employed to reduce mental stress and depression.

So, this small, yellow, sour fruit has proved to be nature's boon to everyone who uses it. It provides many valuable solutions to myriad health-related problems, because it contains its own set of antiseptic and natural medications. A good practice is to eat anywhere from a quarter to a half of a lemon per day to get the maximum benefits from this powerful little fruit! Now, instead of purchasing so many OTC products for all the problems above how much could you save annually? You do the math.

To protect your teeth enamel, wait at least half an hour before brushing your teeth after chewing, drinking or rinsing with lemon juice.

GINGER: Nature's anti-cancer secret

Ginger is one herb that I recommend keeping on hand in your kitchen **AT ALL TIMES**. Not only is it a wonderful addition to your cooking (especially paired with garlic) but it also has enough medicinal properties to fill several books.

http://articles.mercola.com/sites/articles/archive/2014/06/30/ginger-health-benefits.aspx

The National Cancer Institute (NCI) has recently identified ginger as one of the top ten foods offering the highest levels of anti-cancer activity.

The author recommends ginger to everyone for a healthy lifestyle. He personally uses a powerful, organic extract called GingerForce, from the New Chapter Company's line of nutrients. "It features the world's most potent, full-spectrum ginger extract, at least 250 times the concentration of fresh ginger," and the Coach has taken it daily since 2005.

Although well known as a pleasant tasting cooking spice, it is not so widely known that ginger has been used for thousands of years, worldwide, for its numerous potent healing benefits. Ginger is an especially wonderful ally because its healing benefits are particular to so many of our daily health concerns. Probably best known as a superb digestive aid and nausea reliever, ginger also helps heal ulcers, supports cardiovascular health, reduces pain and inflammation, and speeds recovery from colds and flu while reducing fevers. Most importantly, ginger accomplishes all these **without the side effects associated with drugs**.

When Paul Schulick, master herbalist and founder/CEO of New Chapter, www.NewChapter.com began his review of ginger research, both its breadth and depth amazed him. Ginger's benefits are so varied and valuable that Paul regards it as a true "superherb." From this research, Paul's best-selling book Ginger: Common Spice and Wonder Drug was born and with it New Chapter's ginger products.

New Chapter has a 74-acre organic ginger farm, Luna Nueva, that rests on the edge of the beautiful, pristine Children's Rain Forest in Costa Rica. This farm radiates a lushness and vibrancy that reflects a commitment to environmental preservation. While establishing a farm of this kind was challenging, Paul felt it was essential to the quality of his products. He stated that most commercial ginger is heavily fumigated, and he needed a consistent, superior-quality supply of organic ginger.

Ginger's numerous valuable health benefits:

- Supports healthy digestion, offering 180 times the protein digesting power of papaya
- Soothes digestion
- Contains at least 12 anti-aging constituents that inactivate free radicals
- Supports blood platelet health and cardiovascular function
- Enhances natural resistance for cold and flu
- Fights & reduces inflammation
- Enhances natural resistance for cold and flu
- Eases joint pain and fights internal infection and external sores.
- Twenty-two known constituents inhibit inflammatory 5-lipoxygenase, supports prostate health
- May increase absorption and utilization of other nutrients and herbs by as much as 2 to 2.5 times

Ginger Shows Promise as a Cancer and Diabetes Fighter

Ginger's anti-inflammatory properties no doubt make it beneficial for many chronic inflammatory diseases including cancer. Indeed, research published in the British Journal of Nutrition has demonstrated the in vitro and in vivo anticancer activity of ginger, suggesting it may be effective in the management of prostate cancer.

Other research shows it has anti-tumor activity that may help defeat difficult-to-treat types of cancer, including lung, ovarian, colon, breast, skin, and pancreatic. Furthermore, because ginger helps prevent the toxic effects of many substances (including cancer drugs), it may be useful to take in addition to conventional cancer treatments.

As for diabetes, ginger appears to be useful both preventively and therapeutically via effects on insulin release and action, and improved carbohydrate and lipid metabolism.

According to one comprehensive review, a clinical trial that was performed found that after consuming three grams of dry ginger powder for 30 days, diabetic participants had a significant reduction in blood glucose, triglyceride, total cholesterol, and LDL cholesterol. It is thought that ginger has a positive effect on diabetes because it:

- Inhibits enzymes in carbohydrate metabolism
- Increases insulin release and sensitivity
- Improves lipid profiles

Ginger also has also been established to have a protective effect against diabetes complications, including offering protection to the diabetic's liver, kidneys, central nervous system, and eyes.

While ginger has myriad uses all year round and many people wisely eat a few thin slices a day, it is especially useful in summer. As pores open in the heat, cold energy enters the body, causing common problems like the common cold and aching joints. Too much iced foods and beverages aggravate the energy imbalance inside the body, causing problems for the stomach and spleen, such as diarrhea and indigestion.

Spending time in air-conditioned rooms and drinking icy beverages are common in summer, but a cool environment, inside and out, also provides opportunities of pathogenic cold to invade the body. Ginger tea helps dispel pathogenic cold as it is a warm-energy herb and is especially helpful in summer to treat conditions caused by spending too much time in air-conditioned rooms.

Apart from expelling "cold" invasion, ginger can also help defend the body against bacteria since it has antimicrobial properties. Because bacteria reproduce quickly in summer, acute stomach or intestine inflammation is a problem for many people.

Eating some ginger or drinking ginger tea has an antibiotic effect and helps kill salmonella. Serving ginger with seafood is a common practice in China and Japan.

Gargling with a ginger solution can also help relieve bad breath and gum inflammation.

Truly a benchmark in the industry, superlative certified organic softgels, ginger capsules, extracts and syrups are unequaled in their purity and potency.

Unfortunately, a majority of today's corporate scientists working for fortune 500 pharmaceutical companies tend to ignore these naturally healing herbs as much as possible and help to "push" the toxic pharmaceutically manufactured drugs that does little more than treat effects with effects. In fact, these corporate giants have even been caught time and again faking thousands of studies to fraudulently demonstrate the supposed value of pharmaceutical drugs — many of which are later forced by the courts to pay millions in fines, but we aren't idiots and we know all the fine adds up to is nothing but a slap on their collective wrists.

Profits that are threatened by the many real studies that were performed by scientists examining the rejuvenating power of cheap ingredients like turmeric, for example, which has been found by peer-reviewed research available on PubMed to positively influence over 590 conditions. It is great news that those types of studies are bringing the beneficial effects of inexpensive and near-free plant compounds to light. However, there is still a long way to go to slay the big pharmaceutical dragon. So, why wait? Instead, just get your hands on some fresh ginger, or Gingerforce for yourself.

COCONUT OIL: Secrets You Didn't Know

Our understanding of fats and oils, what is healthy and what isn't has been greatly changing over the past few years and decades. One of the products that has generated a lot of questions and interest is coconut oil. Today it has become one of the most popular superfoods and recommended oils for raw and cooked consumption. With this product's increased popularity came many brands with wide ranging quality. It seems everyone wants a piece of this market's share.

Actually, there was a time, the oil was popular in western countries like the United States and Canada, but there was a strong propaganda campaign in the 1970s spread by the corn oil and soy oil industry against coconut oil. Coconut oil was considered harmful for the human body due to its high saturated fat content until the last decade (2000s) when people began to question the claims of the propaganda.

The health benefits of coconut oil are extraordinary, including hair care, skin care, stress relief, cholesterol level maintenance, weight loss, boosted immune system, proper digestion and regulated metabolism. It also provides relief from kidney problems, heart diseases, high blood pressure, diabetes, HIV, and cancer, while helping to improve dental quality and bone strength. These benefits of oil can be attributed to the presence of lauric acid, capric acid and caprylic acid, and their respective properties, such as antimicrobial, antioxidant, anti-fungal, antibacterial and soothing qualities.

It turns out everything about these tasty seeds is pretty great! Yes, coconuts, with their tough exterior rinds are considered seeds.

Offering a myriad of health benefits, coconut oil is affordable, readily available and completely natural. So here is a little information to inspire you to check out this amazing oil!

By regularly massaging your head with coconut oil, you can ensure that your scalp is free of dandruff, even if your scalp is chronically dry. It also helps in keeping your hair and scalp free from lice and lice eggs.

If that weren't enough, coconut oil also reduces the work load on the liver and prevents the accumulation of fat; it helps dissolve kidney stones.

Unrefined coconut oil is a non-hydrogenated, cholesterol free and trans fat-free product. It is rich in medium-chain fatty acids, which are broken down efficiently by the body, providing an immediate source of energy. This is one of the biggest differences in what sets it apart from other saturated fats, making this an optimally healthy saturated fat. It has been linked to aiding numerous health conditions, including Alzheimer's and has numerous beneficial properties like being anti-bacterial. See the following article I wrote, for a full overview of the benefits of coconut oil.

Its flavor, aroma, versatility and health benefits are all outstanding. It is one of the best oils to use for cooking, as it does not denature into harmful compounds at high heat. It can be used as a spread, in cooking, baking and makes outstanding raw, vegan desserts.

To add to its already impressive benefits, coconut oil can also be used topically on our skin and hair. Instead of soaking ourselves with synthetic lotions, full of questionable ingredients, coconut oil can be easily used on the face and body to nourish and moisturize our skin. It can also nourish our scalp and hair, and be used as a massage oil. It absorbs quickly and nurtures our skin exceptionally well.

In lieu of your regular lotion, coconut oil delivers a refreshing, healing, burst of moisture that penetrates your skin and works to truly heal it (not just soak in and dry up!) It can feel oily at first, but that's why it's important to only use a little-it goes a long way. Give it a minute and it will dry beautifully. Use as you would regular lotion.

You can use it on your entire scalp/head for deep conditioning, but you can generally just use it on your ends, where it's the hardest for the body's natural oils to reach, and where the most breakage occurs.

Coconut Oil is Fantastic at Burning Fat

Coconut oil seems to be everywhere these days, from adding new shine to old furniture to producing the best movie popcorn, and now this: just adding two tablespoons of coconut oil to your diet daily, will help you shed belly fat. You'll start noticing a more whittled waistline, and who doesn't want that? A slimmer, more toned physique could be yours and all because of the natural, healthy oil that comes from the humble coconut.

When respected publications like Shape.com and television's Dr. Oz are raving about coconut oil burning belly fat, then we've found a true winner.

Let's take a closer look. Coconut oil is unique because it's a tropical fat that doesn't clog arteries. Coconut oil is comprised of lauric acid fat, which behaves differently in the body. This saturated fat is rich in antibacterial elements as well as anti-oxidant power. Lauric acid encourages enzymes to quickly break down fat cells, so this is beneficial to the body in several ways.

Cooking with coconut oil is easy and flavorful. You can substitute it for butter or any of your other favorite oils like olive, when looking to get your two tablespoon amount in daily. It's wonderful to roast vegetables in, bake goodies with and even make your own mayonnaise. Some enjoy coconut oil in their morning cup of joe. As long as you embark on healthier eating habits and moderate exercise, then two tablespoons of coconut oil to replace other fats is a very good thing for trimming your waistline.

Weight Loss

Coconut oil and weight loss-what's really going on? Well, if you sit around eating coconut oil, you aren't going to lose weight. However, if used to substitute other fats, it can help you drop the pounds by taking the place of those other calories. Unlike most saturated fats, it's mainly comprised of medium chain fatty acids, versus long chain fatty acids. This difference in molecular structure means that it doesn't get packed away as fat as easily and instead is sent straight to the liver to be metabolized, giving you a boost in energy. This energy in turn makes exercising easier, and the exercise in turn helps you lose weight. Another major factor that it plays is as an appetite suppressant. Craving something you shouldn't be? Have a tablespoon or 2 of coconut oil, and that sensation won't last long!

Organic virgin coconut oil is suggested when dropping pounds because zero chemicals have been used to process the oil, plus the micro-nutrients have been preserved. For best results in shedding pounds, the right time to consume coconut oil is about 30 minutes before a meal, because coconut oil makes you feel fuller.

To liquefy, mix 1 tablespoon of coconut oil in a mug and add hot water or herbal tea. Stir to melt and drink. Do this twice a day. If you aren't cuckoo for coconut like that, then simply use it in cooking.

The magic number of two tablespoons comes from a closely watched study showing that one to two tablespoons of coconut oil per day would increase the energy expenditure by 5%, a total of about 120 calories per day. Coconut oil is fantastic at burning fat.

Blood Sugar and Insulin Levels

This tropical fat can help diabetics with blood sugar regulation and eliminate hunger and cravings. Coconut oil is the only healthy oil that diabetics can eat safely, says author of The Coconut Oil Miracle Dr. Bruce Fife:

"Not only does it not contribute to diabetes, but it helps regulate blood sugar, thus lessening the effects of the disease."

Coconut Oil Is Beneficial For Your Thyroid Health

Thyroid problems can present themselves in many ways. You may be feel tired and sluggish, experience weight loss or gain, mood swings, brittle nails and a number of other symptoms. Standard medical treatments such as prescription medications may not suffice. An alternative, natural remedy is available: coconut oil.

What is the thyroid?

The thyroid produces hormones that regulate metabolism, body temperature, the body's use of vitamins and the growth of tissue. A thyroid problem will usually fall into one of two categories:hypothyroidism or hyperthyroidism.

- Hypothyroidism occurs when the thyroid doesn't produce enough of the hormone, so metabolism slows.
- Hyperthyroidism occurs when there is an abundance of the hormone being produced, causing the body's processes to speed up. In the United States, nearly 20 million Americans have some form of thyroid dysfunction, many of them unaware of their problem. The majority of these individuals are women.

REFERENCE - http://positivemed.com/2016/03/21/coconut-oil-daily

Used by Athletes

Coconut oil is often used by athletes, body builders and by those who are dieting. The reason behind this being that coconut oil contains less calories than other oils, its fat content is easily converted into energy, and it does not lead to accumulation of fat in the heart and arteries. Coconut oil helps boost energy and endurance, and generally enhances the performance of athletes.

Healthy Wood Polish

Most wood polish coats surfaces in a slick layer of synthetic chemicals, which makes the wood look all sleek and shiny…for a little bit. Coconut oil, on the other hand, sinks into the wood and keeps it looking "healthy" longer. The appearance is much more natural, and it stays that way. It may not look as dramatic as a store bought polisher, but I find it a much more pleasant and effective option to keeping wood looking it's best.

Lower Cholesterol and Risk of Heart Disease

Cholesterol is a waxy substance found your cells, which helps continuously build more vital cells. It goes about its way through your blood stream attached to proteins known as lipoproteins. There are low-density lipoproteins (LDL) and high-density lipoproteins (HDL.) HDL is the "good" cholesterol-you want to lower LDL, but raise HDL. LDL carries cholesterol throughout your body and delivers it to organs and tissues. The problem is, if you have too much cholesterol, the excess keeps circulating. The constantly circulating LDL will eventually penetrate blood vessel walls where they build up plaques and narrow blood vessels, sometimes to the point blocking blood flow, causing coronary artery disease. HDL, on the other hand, picks up excess cholesterol and brings it to your liver to be broken down. Coconut oil, probably due to its high levels of lauric acid, will boost HDL. There's no solid evidence saying that coconut oil alone will prevent heart disease, but there is solid evidence that it boosts HDL, therefore lowering cholesterol, and hypothetically reducing the risk of heart disease. Take ½ to 1 tablespoon daily.

Oil/Butter Replacement

There's no better way to get the benefits of coconut oil than to replace other less desirable fats with it. When cooking or baking, substitute it for butter or just about any oil. It lends moisture, freshness, and richness to baked goods, and a subtle complimentary flavor to savory dishes. How much you substitute will depend on the recipe you are making. For baking, most people will fall in the 1:1 ratio or 80% coconut oil 20% water when subbing for butter. For basic cakes, cookies, and brownies I find 1:1 to be sufficient. When it comes to more complex pastries that get their flaky puffiness when steam is escaping, you may find yourself tweaking the amount a little. For oil substituting, subbing 1:1 is a good route to go.

SPF Lip Balm

Lips are quite exposed to the elements, and it's not like there are "lip scarves" or "mouth mittens" to protect them from the harsh world. One thing that's especially over-looked is sun exposure. You should really apply sunscreen to your lips for full protection, but coconut oil also has a mild SPF protection. It can't rival SPF 80 (indeed it has an SPF of about 4-6) but even that little bit can help. Apply some coconut oil just before heading out into the sun, and reapply every few hours. I like to melt mine down with just ¼ teaspoon or so of beeswax, as I find it easier to apply, and it has more staying power.

Exfoliating Body Scrub

One of my personal favorite uses for coconut oil is serving as a base for body or face scrubs. You can melt some down, stir in some sugar, let it cool, and then use as is. Or, for a fun little project, melt down about a half cup of coconut oil and pour into a muffin tin, soap mold, or anything of the like, and stir in 2-4 tablespoons of white or brown sugar. You can add more if you would like the texture to be coarser. I usually let it cool some before adding the sugar so you don't just dissolve the grains. Pop it in the fridge and let it solidify and cool completely before removing from the mold. Slice off a piece when needed and use it to gently scrub and exfoliate your face/body (dampen your skin with water first.) Rinse off, apply moisturizer, and resist the urge to use it again until later in the week, otherwise you run the risk of drying your skin out.

Make-Up Remover:

Make-up is on your face. Your face is something you would like to protect. So when it comes to removing make-up, don't turn for harsher store bought products. Go instead to coconut oil, which gently and safely removes all traces of make-up (and leaves your face feeling healthy and refreshed.) Simply scoop some onto your fingertips (it will melt quickly as you use it) and rub it over make-up in a circular motion, rinsing with water afterwards to remove traces of makeup and patting your face dry. It works well with eye make-up, waterproof or not, as well. You can use a mild soap if you wish to remove all traces of the oil.

Massage Oil

The benefits of massage are countless, and we could all use one now and again. Rather than using a heavy lotion, simply use coconut oil. You can add essential oils for scent if you like, but I find the smell of coconut oil alone to be heavenly. It also leaves your skin truly moisturized and soft.

Nail and Cuticle Treatment

Cuticles get raggedy, nails get broken, chipped, or dull, and it's not unusual for them to need some TLC every now and then. While there is a plethora of store-bought creams designed specially to miraculously make them look ready for a photo shoot, they are typically over-priced and filled with weird ingredients. This is where coconut oil comes in. Rub a little into your cuticles and over/around your nails to help smooth out flaws and encourage healthy growth.

Deodorant

Sweat on its own typically **DOES NOT** smell. In fact, most sweat doesn't smell at all, since most sweat glands on our body are eccrine, which produces mostly water with some salt and maybe some uric acid. Apocrine sweat glands become active during puberty, and produce sweat from our underarms, around the genitals, etc. The sweat from apocrine glands has other stuff in it, such as lipids (fats.) When the bacteria on our skin feed on these fats, the byproducts smell. Like store-bought deodorant, coconut oil helps decrease the bacteria count that's causing the odor. Mix about a tablespoon of arrowroot powder into 3-4 tablespoons of coconut oil for an easy homemade deodorant. Apply as needed; adding beeswax to solidify it some if you feel the coconut oil is too thin on its own.

Bath Oil

Soften your bath water, and your skin, with a bit of coconut oil. Enjoy its lovely aroma and gently swish it around now and then to swirl it through the water. It will naturally coat your skin, leaving it smooth and healthy.

Just imagine having one hundred-sixty (160) uses of coconut oil. See the link below for the full list. Coach Melvin uses two types of coconut oil: unrefined, and virgin. The unrefined coconut oil in place of hair conditioner, lotion, insect repellent, and it can be used on cellulite, ear infection, athletes foot, back pain, sore muscles, and even as **FURNITURE POLISH**! The organic, virgin coconut oil is used for cooking, baking, in place of butter on toast, a spoonful in a smoothie, on various types of food, etc. A teaspoonful on rice with chicken along with soy sauce is exceptionally delicious. So, again, just imagine the hundreds of dollars you can save annually just by replacing many of your OTC products you normally purchase, with coconut oil. Lastly, the following types are an example of how to use them:

PURPOSE	PREFERABLE TYPE TO BUY
Cooking	Refined Coconut Oil
Weight Loss	Virgin Coconut Oil
As a Carrier Oil	Virgin Coconut Oil, Fractionated Coconut Oil
Good Health	Virgin Coconut Oil, Organic Coconut Oil
Hair	Pure Coconut Oil Refined Coconut Oil
Medicinal uses	Virgin Coconut Oil, Virgin Organic Coconut Oil

Source:

www.organicfacts.net/health-benefits/oils/health-benefits-of-coconut-oil.html

PAPAYA: Packed with extraordinary power

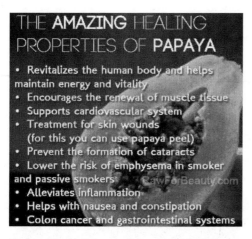

THE AMAZING HEALING PROPERTIES OF PAPAYA
- Revitalizes the human body and helps maintain energy and vitality
- Encourages the renewal of muscle tissue
- Supports cardiovascular system
- Treatment for skin wounds (for this you can use papaya peel)
- Prevent the formation of cataracts
- Lower the risk of emphysema in smoker and passive smokers
- Alleviates inflammation
- Helps with nausea and constipation
- Colon cancer and gastrointestinal systems

Millions of people are actually in the dark regarding the exceptional power and healing benefits of plant life that grows from the earth. The superb healing benefits have been so down-played, and replaced by high-powered multibillion dollar media advertising of junk foods and pharmaceutical drugs, that the world's population have all but forgotten about the effectiveness of plantlife in the treatment of, healing of, and how they were designed and created to maintain and sustain the health of the human body for at least one hundred twenty years.

The author considers papaya to be a super food in that, like many of the other fruits and vegetables, it effectively treats and heals so many different types of ailments. Although fresh papaya is the best, and should be kept and eaten by literally everyone, it is seemingly impractical in this fast-paced, high-tech society we live in. Therefore, I will focus on Digestive Enzyme Supplements.

Papaya enzyme supplements are packed with extraordinary power. They are not only good for your digestive system, these amazing little chewable tablets are also very beneficial for the skin, colds & Flu, promotes healing, and has an even more important role to play when taken on an empty stomach. The primary therapeutic benefit is derived from its enzyme, called papain

The vitamins and nutrients in papaya are exceptional. Papaya is rich in many vitamins, minerals, nutrients and antioxidants including vitamin C, folate, potassium, dietary fiber, vitamin A, vitamin E, vitamin K, carotenes, flavonoids, B vitamins, magnesium and pantothenic acid. Its vitamin concentration works well to help avert the oxidation of cholesterol. When cholesterol is allowed to oxidize, it adheres to and accumulates in the walls of blood vessels. Therefore, this supplement may help ward off atherosclerosis and diabetic heart disease. In addition, the carotenoids, antioxidants and vitamins in papaya can help keep your eyes healthy. As a matter of fact, they may also reduce the risk of macular degeneration, an age-related condition resulting in loss of vision.

So, what else is papaya enzyme good for? Check it out: digestive system, skin, colds & Flu, promotes healing:

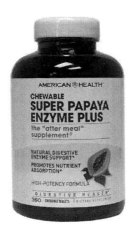

Digestive System

As a useful digestive enzyme, papain helps the stomach to break down protein easily in order to facilitate the absorption of nutrients. Its anti-inflammatory effects also helps soothe the stomach when it is upset. It has been shown to be effective in treating ulcers. Papain has been shown to help in regulating irritable bowel syndrome.

It helps to facilitate proper digestion and dissolves fats, relieving heartburn. The enzymes also have been effective in relieving various food allergies.

Skin (Note: This organ is THE largest of the body.)

Papaya enzymes help to soften the texture of the skin by dissolving various fats.

These enzymes are also helpful in treating swelling and bruising by reducing swelling.

Papain helps to clean the dead cells/tissues in the body, leaving healthy-looking skin.

Papain is also effective in curbing swelling that develops after surgery.

Healing

With its anti-inflammatory effects, it helps:

- reduce the pain and swelling of sprains/strains.
- reduce the swelling and speeds up the healing of burns.
- in the treatment of cold sores.
- promote wound healing, although this has not been scientifically proven as of yet.

The easiest and most convenient way to gain these tremendously effective benefits from papaya is to take it in supplement form. They come conveniently in the form of deliciously chewable tablets (with a taste similar to children's chewable vitamins) that you can carry with you anywhere. However, you can also get it as a powder, which you can mix in nearly any drink. The supplements are generally produced by collecting the latex from the papaya fruit by scoring its neck. The latex is either allowed to dry on the fruit itself or to drip inside a container suspended from the fruit. Following this step, it is allowed to dry until it becomes dry and crude. This is followed by a purification step in order to remove any contaminants from it, and then the purified enzyme is supplied in the form of papain tablets or papain powder.

The above usefulness of papaya enzyme is excellent, but the primary therapeutic benefit is derived from its enzyme, called papain. Papain is a cysteine protease enzyme that is well known for its various digestive health benefits. Papaya has been used for its medicinal benefits since the 18th century, but it wasn't until 1870 when the papain enzyme itself was discovered. Since that time, extensive research has been performed on its health benefits. I, Coach Melvin, have personally used papaya enzyme since 1976.

Coach Melvin is a CHEATER! Many people ask me, "Hey Coach, how is it that you stay so trim and healthy?" Well, ok let me give you a secret. It's a secret I obtained from my friend Dick Gregory (prominent 1960s activist, former well-known comedian, and creator of famed 1980s The Bahamian Diet currently available as Dick Gregory's Caribbean Diet for Optimal Health). So my secret is that **I CHEAT!**

I eat ANYTHING and EVERYTHING I want: cake, cookies, brownies, ice cream, candy, Lay's potato chips, sodas (about 6 liters a week), lots of rice with practically every single meal. And, sometimes I even eat a whole box of cookies in one day. I've been doing this for the past FORTY (40) YEARS! Now, while many of my relatives and contemporaries are obese, many with high blood pressure, diabetes, myriad other negative health issues, and some whom have died because of self-brought-on complications with one or more of their internal organs, why is it that I am in EXCELLENT health with a thriving immune and cardiovascular system, perfectly functioning internal organs, still movin' & groovin', and looking young?

No! It's not because of heredity, which is nothing but an excuse. And, I'm not bragging or anything like that. It is simply because I have been **CONSISTENT** in the following:

- Drinking 8 or more glasses of PURE water daily,
- Exercising (calisthenics, Tai Chi, Kungfu), 2 hours, 3 or 4 days a week,
- Qigong Meditation (chee-gung, chee-kung), about 30 min DAILY,
- Chewing 5 or 6 papaya enzyme tablets both before AND after eating meals and any junk foods (I've done it for about 40 years CONSISTENTLY since 1976),
- Taking an ALL-NATURAL, WHOLE-FOOD vitamin supplement with my main meals (since 1971). The current one I consume is EveryMan II from New Chapter, Inc.,
- Every morning, drinking a warm glass or cup of either: LEMON JUICE squeezed into my water, or pure kosher ORGANIC Opti-MSM crystals, or a cup of organic ginger tea,
- Regarding exercising, I don't necessarily do calisthenics daily, but I practice these three internal martial arts EVERY SINGLE DAY WITHOUT FAIL: Qigong, Tai Chi Chuan, and Baguazhang.

Some things, however, I will in no way partake of; things like drinking alcoholic beverages, hard liquor, smoking cigarettes, cigars, pipes, marijuana or mind-altering recreational drugs. Nor will I sniff or inject toxic drugs such as heroin and the like.

Over the years—and because of Dick Gregory, author of Dick Gregory's Natural Diet for Folks Who Eat: Cookin' With Mother Nature, the author has done extensive research on papaya. The reason why you can "cheat" in your diet is because of some of the components in papaya:

- **Protease** - a proteolytic enzyme effective on meat, seafood, soybean, etc.,
- **Lipase** - a fats-degrading enzyme effect on beef, fresh cream, egg yolk, cheese, etc.,
- **Amylase** - a sugar-degrading enzyme effective on chocolate, cake, biscuits, cookies, soft drinks, and alcohol.

Digestive or metabolic enzymes are found in our saliva and along the gastrointestinal tract. They are involved in the breakdown of food and aid nutrient absorption into the bloodstream and eventually into our cells.

Enzymes help jump-start our digestion process and take some of the stress off of our system to break down the food we consume.

Papaya digestive enzyme supplement helps break down food in the stomach, which can reduce heartburn, acid reflux, and other GI conditions

Age

"Also, as we age, the process of digestion does slow down a bit, so anyone over the age of 65 may benefit from digestive enzyme supplements, but only if there are symptoms."

Digestive discomfort

Some of the most common symptoms are gas, bloating and diarrhea. If you experience any discomfort after your meals, and if you are experiencing these then you should be using papaya enzyme supplements, though it's always a good idea to check with your doctor.*

Take digestive enzymes throughout a meal

As for dosage, "It is more effective if the enzyme is taken at the beginning of a meal as opposed to after because there is less activity and interference from the stomach acid -- but Dick Gregory recommends taking them both before AND after a meal, which is what I do; I love the taste anyway, and since it leaves enzymes in your mouth after you chew the tablets---if you take the chewable ones---it helps the enzymes in your saliva break down foods even more before it slides down to your stomach. If you prefer the capsules, however, you can do this by pulling apart the capsule and mixing some into your beverage or directly onto your food. Wow! How convenient is THAT!

*Talk to an alternative doctor: Osteopathic physician (D.O.), Naturopath physician (ND), Naprapath physician (D.N.), O.M.D. doctor or a doctor of TCM (Traditional Chinese Medicine). Whenever I have the chance, I strongly urge people to seek second or third medical opinions from one or more of the above type of doctors because these doctors are less likely to have a vested interest in the pharmaceutical drug trade like the typical allopathic (M.D.) doctor does.

About digestive enzymes.

Before beginning a digestive enzyme regimen, contact your physician and find out if they are right for you -- there can be mild, non-health threatening side effects associated with taking any type of supplement. If you're having symptoms of digestive distress, however, digestive enzymes might just be the answer for you!

Papaya fruit is a rich source of valuable proteolytic enzymes, such as papain, chymopapain, caricain and glycyl endopeptidase, that can greatly aid in the digestive process. This is especially true of meals that contain meat or other concentrated forms of protein.

But, as this page will show, papaya enzyme can have many other health benefits and may have an even more important role to play when taken on an empty stomach.

Protein Digestion and Papaya Enzymes

Many of us eat large amounts of low quality meat each week that can put great strain on our digestive system and enzyme producing pancreas. Processed meats, with additives such as the potentially carcinogenic sodium nitrite, are particularly worrying from a health perspective.

To make matters worse, rushed meals, extra large serving sizes, low digestive enzymes, stomach acid production, and poorly functioning digestive systems in general all contribute to this meat often ending up only partially digested by the time it reaches the lower intestine.

Here it can putrefy as it is acted upon by masses of bacteria that causes flatulence (in street vernacular, that means farting). But smelly gas is the least of the potential health problems caused by undigested protein in the colon. The place to fix flatulence and other more serious health issues associated with poor digestion, such as constipation, leaky gut syndrome and IBS, is not at the end of the process in the colon, but at the beginning.

Breakdown of other 'troublesome' proteins, such as the gluten in wheat and the casein in milk are often implicated in digestive problems. In our intestines, papain and other papaya enzymes can help clear undigested protein-based debris and waste products.

If fresh papaya is unavailable or too expensive, green papaya capsules can be taken with a meal high in protein and are an easy way to improve its digestion and avoid intestinal problems later on. As you can probably deduce, having the capsules are extremely convenient when you think of the difficulty of always keeping fresh papaya anywhere and everywhere.

Proteolytic enzymes in the bloodstream are known to reduce inflammation in your body, possibly by scavenging damaged and oxidized proteins. These damaged proteins are implicated in a variety of debilitating autoimmune disorders such as severe allergies, chronic fatigue syndrome and a weakened immune system that is much more vulnerable to infections and disease.

Did I forget to mention that you can also have delicious all-natural papaya drinks? Papain and other proteolytic enzymes are also understood to break down fibrin protein, which is involved in both the formation of dangerous blood clots and provides a protective coating for cancer cells. It is this action of potentially dissolving cancerous cells' protective coating that has many experts interested in papain for use in cancer prevention and possibly even as part of a treatment for cancer.

If this was vital and beneficial information to you, remember, the more people you tell about this book, and they in turn purchase it and read it, the more you'll be showing your love for humankind.

Nuts: Not just a holiday treat

It is highly suggested you consider nuts as a part of your *daily* nutrition, not just a staple for the Thanksgiving holiday season. Various nuts are packed with heart-healthy fats, protein, and disease-fighting vitamins and minerals. However, and mostly due to their popularity, a summary of two nuts are given here.

If you want to talk about superfoods **walnuts**, more than any other, holds that enviable position. Why? Walnuts are nutrient-packed, and we're still discovering all the benefits they can bring. A recent study found that walnuts may actually enhance reasoning skills in teenagers!

Considered a high-end nut, much of the walnut's stellar reputation comes from its richness in essential fatty acids, particularly alpha-linolenic and linoleic acid. Another study during 2006, that was well-publicized, showed that the fatty acids derived from regular walnut consumption decreased subjects' total cholesterol level and LDL cholesterol in short-term trials. But don't worry, you don't have to eat a tree's worth to see the benefits!

Just 1/4 cup daily serving provides nearly 100% of the total recommended omega-3 fatty acid intake, with only 163 calories. A 1 oz serving has more omega-3s than a 4 oz piece of salmon. Walnuts also contain phytonutrients and antioxidants known to be helpful in reducing inflammation levels and warding off type 2 diabetes. Oh, and if you ever have trouble sleeping, **just toss the sleeping pills**, as walnuts are a rich source of melatonin, which encourages a healthy sleep cycle.

Almonds, on the other hand, are ubiqutous: in salads, on pizzas, Chinese restaurants (Almond Chicken), as snacks with all manner of seasonings - they even enjoy the enviable position of having their own milk. And, with good reason: almonds rank among the highest-protein nuts, albeit at a fraction of the price you'd pay for some of its higher-end buddies like walnuts. Being high in manganese and vitamin E, they are vital defenders against oxidative damage.

Consuming them on a regular basis puts you at a lower risk for developing heart disease. One study even found they actually help lower elevated cholesterol.

Chapter 16 - Mushrooms: Some of the Most Potent, Natural Medicines on the Planet

Although there can be no doubt as to the effectiveness of all the natural fruits, vegetables, herbs, and nuts listed above, in the healing of the body, mushrooms are incredible and, by most people, not well understood. Therefore, we've dedicated a complete chapter on this "earth gold" to help you expand your horizons and become aware of the healing benefits these *exceptionally* powerful substances provide.

These healing properties have become famous far and wide and one of them, Reishi, is even lauded in the American Herbal Pharmacopoeia and Therapeutic Compendium.

There are myriad types of mushrooms around the world, many are edible, others are not, and some are poisonous. Showcased here, however, are seven (7) of the most potent, edible mushrooms available. They contain antibacterial, antifungal, antiviral, antioxidant and antitumor properties. **Many mushrooms have been shown to stop or even destroy cancer cells in their tracks**. So, read this chapter in its entirety, use it as a reference, and begin your nutrional journey. Your health will love you for it.

The seven mushrooms showcased are:

- Wild Forest Chaga (Mushroom of Immortality)
- Shiitake
- Lions Mane
- Maitake (Hen in the woods)
- Reishi (Tree pancake)

- Cordyceps
- Turkey Tail

First and foremost, we start with one that practically escapes detection because it does not have the shape or form of the typical mushroom. However, it exudes practically life-saving substances, making it a superfood.

Introducing....

Wild Forest Chaga

(King of All Herbs; Mushroom of Immortality; The "Gift from God")

Rather than soft like a mushroom, chaga is hard, almost as hard as wood, resembles a lump of coal, and **has the highest antioxidant value of any food on earth**, as measured by the ORAC scale. It is unique, nothing like common mushrooms. In fact, chaga is the most nutritionally dense of all tree growths. Known by the Siberians as the "Gift from God" and the "Mushroom of Immortality," this vibrant growth has been used by humans to support health for thousands of years. The Japanese call it "The Diamond of the Forest," while the Chinese deem it "King of Plants." For the Chinese that is saying a lot, since they have an immense history with countless plants. This may be why documented use of chaga exists as early as 100 BC in the **Shen Nong Ben Cao Jing — the foundation of traditional Chinese medicine**, www.traditionalstudies.org/shen-nong-ben-cao-division-of-herbs

- Chaga is a non-toxic, parasitic medicinal mushroom with anti-cancer properties. It grows in birch forests in harsh northern latitudes — the kinds of places we associate with freezing to death fast, not "immortality."
- In China, Siberia, Finland, Japan, and Poland, ancient and native peoples have long known about the benefits of chaga.

- Older Asians use it for healthy natural balance. It is thought to support the life force or life energy—chi (also spelled qi and pronounced "chee"). They believe consuming this mushroom extends youthfulness, prolongs life, and enhances immunity.

- To get more scientific, chaga (Inonotus obliquus) is unusual among mushrooms. Instead of gills or caps, the chaga has pores. And, the inside is a brownish-yellow cork-like mass with beige veins. Its use has been documented in the oldest surviving official list of medicinal substances — the Chinese book **Sennong Ben Cao Jing**, which is 2,300 years old.

Call it folk medicine if you will, but modern science suggests the ancients were on to an amazing secret. Isn't it time you got in on it too? Let's take a look:

To survive in harsh climates, chaga concentrates natural compounds for its protection, and that is why it is so powerful. To strengthen the tree, as well as heal, it makes potent phytochemicals, including sterols, phenols, and enzymes. Researchers have inoculated sick trees with chaga to strengthen them. People benefit greatly by consuming these forest-source phytochemicals and nutrients.

Nutrient dense

Chaga is one of the most potent whole-food complexes on earth, because it contains virtually every known nutrient in significant quantities. Because of their special, biologically potent substances, trees live long, far longer than herbs. Some trees live as long as 10,000 years or more. Thus, they are the most powerful living beings in the world. Concentrating this power, chaga contains numerous B vitamins, flavonoids, phenols, minerals, and enzymes. It is also one of the world's densest sources of pantothenic acid, and this vitamin is needed by the adrenal glands as well as digestive organs. It also contains riboflavin and niacin in significant amounts.

In particular, it is highly rich in special phenols which are pigment-like. These phenolic compounds are known as chromogenic complex. Chaga can be up to 30% chromogenic complex by weight. The chromogenic complex is highly protective for all tissues and is only found in chaga. In the cream base this chromogenic complex is hightly protective of the skin. Rubbed on the skin it even helps people develop a tan, because it contains the pigment melanin, the same pigment responsible for dark-colored skin.

Chaga contains wild-source minerals and is particularly high in copper, calcium, potassium, manganese, zinc, and iron. Yet, its most potent ingredient is a special substance known as superoxide dismutase (SOD). This is an enzyme with great potency. Its function is to halt oxidation, especially the toxicity of a free radical known as singlet oxygen. This is the type of oxygen which is responsible for oxidizing and damaging the tissues, which results in aging. It is the same oxygen which rusts a nail. SOD blocks this damage by quenching the singlet oxygen free radical. The SOD content per gram of chaga is exceedingly high and accounts for many of its historical powers. Tests performed on North American Herb & Spice's wild chaga prove that it contains some 10,000 to 20,000 active SOD units per gram. This is an exceedingly high amount, far higher than that found even in typical SOD pills. The typical SOD pill contains from 200 to 2,000 units per serving. So the difference is considerable. Plus, the type in pills is virtually impossible to absorb, while the wild chaga type is well-utilized by the body.

Ancient Chinese regarded it as a longevity factor

Yet, here is the main thing you need to know. Chaga is a health food which supports the entire internal system of your body. The Siberians drink it daily. This is why they are long-lived. The chaga drinker lives 85 to 100 years, while the non chaga-drinking person, the Inuit, lives only about 50 years. This proves that natural phytochemicals, the ones found in chaga, do make a difference. Yet, there is more traditional use that offers evidence. Ancient Chinese regarded it as a longevity factor, which is why they deemed it the most complete of all growths. Japanese and Koreans use it regularly, and look how powerful they are today. In much of Siberia, Russia, and Eastern Europe it is an essential beverage. Unfortunately, our U.S. government restricts me from making medical claims, but here is what I AM able to say: **Chaga has been used as an essential whole food supplement for many years by Russia's long-lived peasants, as well as long-lived villagers of Japan and Korea. These village people consume it as a daily beverage. They prefer it over common drinks such as tea and coffee. Because of its cleansing properties, in primitive Siberia the chaga drink was known as "soup water," although its taste is a pleasant combination of tea and coffee.**

Chaga is validated by Moscow's Medical Academy of Science

In his book The Cancer Ward, Alexander Solzhenitzyn wrote about the health benefits of chaga. His character in the novel took it with positive results. Regardless, chaga was then validated by Moscow's Medical Academy of Science, 1955, and was extensively used by the public. It is one of Russia's state secrets for power and strength and was heavily used by champion Russian athletes, who defeated all others, including the best teams America could offer. So, the Russians, Siberians, Poles, Romanians, Koreans, Japanese, and Chinese all use it. This alone shows the importance for Americans regarding this essential whole food.

Here is what the Russians discovered. They determined that certain plants help your body fight the effects of stress and disease. They called these plants adaptogens. They discovered that chaga is the most potent adaptogen known. This is why it is the basis for the fight against premature aging and for prevention of serious diseases. Now you too can experience the health benefits of wild chaga, the plant responsible for the exceptional health and long life of the Siberian tribes-people.

Wild chaga was found to be the most powerful adaptogen

Since the 1950s the government of the Union of Soviet Socialist Republics (USSR), in conjunction with approximately 1,200 prominent scientists, conducted over 3,000 experiments involving half a million (500,000) people to study the effects of adaptogens. An adaptogen is a substance which modifies the human body's response to stress. The results of these studies were a protected Soviet secret for 40 years. The Soviet government commanded athletes, astronauts and other Soviet elite to take adaptogens on a daily basis to improve physical and mental work capacity. One of these adaptogens was chaga. In fact, of all these adaptogens, chaga was found to be the most powerful. It is now believed that up to 80% of all diseases are mainly due to stress.

Chaga is available in various and unique forms

Chaga is available in several forms, including sublingual emulsified drops, a chaga-birch bark tea (with purple maca), a pleasant, ready-to-drink beverage in an 8-ounce bottle, a delicious chocolate-like syrup, and face or body cream. Be sure to get the original chaga, which is truly wild and free of all chemicals and solvents. Get the power of wild, far northern nature. Get NAHS wild-harvested chaga. Accept no chaga imitations made commercially in labs—only buy real, wild forest chaga. "King of Herbs," "Mushroom of Immortality," "Diamond of the Forest," "King of Plants," and "Gift of God" say it all and only apply to truly wild chaga. This forest complex is truly incredible. A simple cup or two of this tea has a dramatic effect—without any stimulants. No matter which chaga product you take, you can feel the difference immediately. With NAHS chaga supplements, it is the real kind—not the vat-grown type from labs.

Unless it is the truly wild kind, as used exclusively by North American Herb & Spice, it can't even be called chaga. Never be fooled. Get only the real chaga with North American Herb & Spice's exclusive handpicked, handmade, wild chaga supplements.

Chaga gives you the strength that you need to function throughout the day

Relax with a cup of chaga beverage, or experience the power of the raw chaga drops under the tongue. Soothe yourself with the wild, raw chaga experience. Get the strength you need to make it through the day and much more. Feel the power of the wild forest though North American Herb & Spice's chaga.

Experience the immense power of wild birch tree power. This is the energy and power of wild-source enzymes, notably SOD, peroxidase, and nucleases, as well as wild sterols, phenols, B vitamins, minerals, and much more. Take advantage of it for you, your loved ones, and anyone else in need.

It is one of the most praised superfoods.

Among other health benefits, chaga tea is one of the richest sources of antioxidants in the world, containing not only some of the highest levels but also an exceptionally rare diversity of antioxidants. It is also alkalizing and an "adaptogen," meaning that it works with your body's unique constitution to bring you back toward balance. Chaga has been used for thousands of years by people in Siberia, Russia and other parts of Asia. As a matter of fact, the emperor of China once outlawed chaga, as he wanted exclusive use of this age-defying tonic so that he could appear eternally "young" while everyone around him grew old!

Chaga is known to many as the King of the forest. It stands a unique role in the ecosystem and is a catalyst of the complex and elaborate life force of the forest.

This super-charged mushroom that grows over the course of many years on living birch trees sucking the life force and medicine out of it and making it bio-available to us humans, is unlike most other tree mushrooms; chaga grows on **living** trees.

Although chaga has been used without problems for thousands of years, you should be aware of two possible drug interactions, given today's culture where millions are on pharmaceutical drugs. Here are two warnings before you use chaga:

1. Chaga magnifies the effects of anti-clotting drugs like aspirin and warfarin (so-called blood thinners). So if you are on those, consult with your doctor before using chaga. A wide range of supplements are blood thinners, including fish oil and digestive enzymes, but this is not a big deal. If your doctor is cooperative and not biased toward nutritional healing substances, he should be willing to let you reduce or possibly even eliminate the pharmaceutical blood thinner because **the natural supplement will do the job**.
2. Chaga also interacts with diabetes medications like insulin. It thereby raises your risk of hypoglycemia (low blood sugar), and could send your blood sugar levels into free fall.

If you're not on these drugs, however, everything we've found suggests clear sailing.

Shiitake

The most well documented benefits of shiitake mushrooms are on the immune system. They act like an adaptogen, able to either boost immune activity or prevent excessive immune activity, depending on the body's needs.

Antiviral, antibacterial, antitumor and antifungal properties: Some studies suggest that shiitake can help protect against cardiovascular disease. This may be due to their antioxidant power in the cardiovascular system.

Animal studies done at the National University of Singapore showed that tumors either stopped growing or shrunk significantly in mice with human colon-carcinoma cells.

How to eat them:

Shiitake is a meaty rich-flavored mushroom and can be eaten raw or cooked in various dishes. For better flavor, they can first be briefly soaked in water or sautéd.

Lions Mane

Lions Mane mushrooms look kind of wacky, with cascading tendrils that resemble a lion's mane. They have been used for thousands of years in Asia and are said to give one "nerves of steel and the memory of a lion." It is thought Buddhist monks also used Lions Mane to enhance brain power and their ability to concentrate during meditation

Lions Mane is said to be the top super mushroom for the brain and nervous system. In fact animal studies have been done to test its ability to aid nerve regeneration, with promising results. It is believed to be helpful for those with epilepsy or other seizure related disorders and Alzheimer's disease.

Lions mane was discovered by Dr. Hirokazu Kawagishi in Japan to stimulate Nerve Growth Factor, which is the protein that enhances and repairs neurological disorders. It is responsible for brain tissue regeneration and memory, and is also thought to help with elevating one's mood.

In Chinese medicine, lions mane is used to help stomach and digestive issues like ulcers and gastritis.

Antioxidant properties: Lions mane contains high amounts of antioxidants, which are made available when the mushrooms are heated. They are also full of polysaccharides and polypeptides that work to enhance the immune system.

How to eat them:

Using powdered extracts of Lion's Mane is the most effective way to receive all the medicinal benefits from the mushroom. The powder is also available in capsule form. It can be taken like a pill, added to hot drinks, shakes, or smoothies. It is also available in tincture form. Depending on where you live, you might be able to find whole dried mushrooms that you can use for tea, or fresh mushrooms that you can steam.

Lions mane has a firm texture and can easily be **used as a meat replacement**.

Maitake

Maitake, "the dancing mushroom", is native to the mountains of Japan. According to legend, it was once so rare that people would dance for joy when they found it, as it was worth its own weight in silver. In Italy they call it "the unmarried woman" while in America we call it "hen of the woods". This is probably because it looks like a fluffed up chicken sitting at the base of trees.

Health Benefits:

Maitake is thought to help reduce the risk of Type 2 Diabetes because it regulates blood sugar levels. Diabetes is responsible for numerous other health issues like neuropathy, kidney disease, weight problems and retina degeneration. In one study, diabetic mice who took maitake powder had decreased blood sugar levels while no change happened in the control group.

A small study in Japan showed that maitake can help with polycystic ovary syndrome (PCOS). PCOS can cause infertility, irregular periods and other complications. Taking maitake regularly helped those with PCOS have an ovulation rate of 77%. Although taking certain medications can create the same or better outcomes, they also come with undesirable side effects. Maitake has none.

Anti-cancer and antiviral properties: Maitake can be a powerful immune system booster. Several studies point to maitake as stimulating apoptosis, or "programmed suicide", of cancer cells as well as stopping the proliferation of blood that feeds tumors.

How to eat them:

You can find dried maitake mushrooms sold online or in most asian stores. Certain elements of maitake are common in supplement form. You can also cook raw mushrooms yourself with organic butter (or ghee), or throw them in soups and salads.

Reishi (The Pancake Mushroom)

Reishi mushrooms were used for food and medicine as far back as the reign of the first Chinese emperor. The Chinese even believed in a 'Reishi Goddess' that bestowed health, youth, and longevity. Historically it was only given to royalty. Even today it is one of the most respected mushrooms in China, Japan, Korea, and other Asian countries.

Health Benefits: Everyone who takes Reishi notices the peacefulness that seems to accompany its use. Many people are able to stop using chemical drugs.

Reishi has been said to be a "fix-it-all" mushroom for issues such as diabetes, heart problems asthma, ulcers, fatigue, insomnia, high cholesterol, etc.

An ingredient in reishi called triterpenes may help with common allergies by blocking histamine release and helping the body use oxygen.

Reishi mushrooms are also known as adaptogens, and can aid all the organs of the body in creating homeostasis (balance). It is also thought to 'fine tune' the immune system.

Antibacterial, antiviral, antifungal, antioxidant and anti-inflammatory properties: Certain enzymes in reishi mushrooms help to rid the body of toxins and free radicals, as well as help the liver. Out of 204 mushrooms tested in Spain for their antimicrobial properties against certain bacterias, reishi ranked at the top of the list. An antimicrobial is something that kills microorganisms in the body.

Although reishi has yet to be proved as a treatment for cancer, researchers agree it is at least a beneficial supplement for those enduring chemotherapy and radiation.

How to eat them:

Reishi mushrooms are traditionally prepared as teas or infusions. They can also be found in capsules and tinctures. Recently they've become an ingredient in energy drinks and certain coffee blends. They are difficult to eat raw because their skin is so tough.

There are different varieties, however, having different colours going to about six (6): Akashiba (red reishi), Kuroshiba (black reishi), Aoshiba (blue reishi), Kishiba (yellow reishi), Shiroshiba (white reishi), and Murasakishiba (purple reishi).

Therapeutic Benefits of Reishi

Scientific studies have shown that the Reishi mushroom has properties that contribute to the healing of tumours, lowering of blood sugar and cholesterol levels. Laboratory tests have  confirmed that the mushroom has extracts that fight some kinds of cancer. These cancers include epithelial ovarian cancer. When tested on an animal, Reishi was found to work just like the Shiitake mushroom in preventing cancer metastasis.

The stage when Reishi mushroom fights cancer best is yet to be specified. It is established though, that it may inhibit fresh formation of tumour induced blood capillaries or veins. This has the impact of cutting food supply to the tumour and curtailing perpetual growth. It may also inhibit movement of cancer cells within the body. It has the potential also to hinder the cancer cells' ability to multiply. Currently, extracts from the Reishi mushroom are in use commercially in pharmaceuticals. The medication made and sold in these pharmaceuticals is geared towards suppressing the proliferation and spread of cancer cells. MC-S is one such pharmaceutical company.

In addition to fighting cancer, Reishi is also considered important in reversion of viral activity, regulating cardiovascular activity, fighting against chronic fatigue, rheumatoid arthritis, and helping diabetes patients. These areas, however, have limited clinical tests to support them.

Low immunity levels can make people vulnerable, not only to things like viral or bacterial infections, but also to serious conditions like cancer, since the body is unable to recognize and eliminate cancer cells in the early stages of their development, before they can become established in the body and proliferate.

Reishi mushrooms work within the body in a number of ways, not only to help strengthen the body's own natural defenses, but also against specific cancer cells themselves to keep people healthy and to reduce or eliminate cancer at its onset.

Helps treats inflammatory breast cancer

Inflammatory breast cancer (IBC) is a very difficult form of cancer to deal with because it is pervasive and likely to spread to other parts of the body. Reishi mushrooms can improve this condition because they have an inhibitory effect on the reproduction of the cancer cells and also because they have powerful anti-inflammatory properties.

Prevents secondary infections

Cancer patients not only have to deal with the immediate problems of their disease, but also with the fact that, because their immune system is weakened, they are also vulnerable to secondary infections from bacteria, viruses, fungi and other pathogens. Reishi mushrooms help prevent these issues by strengthening the body's immune response.

Modulates the immune system

Reishi mushrooms have been proven to have immunomodulatory effects: Active compounds in these mushrooms can not only break down the fibrogen in the outer, protective layer of cancer cells and make them more easily eliminated but also help amplify the activity of the natural killer cells, the body's way of fighting against pathogens directly.

Effective for ovarian cancer

In one study to research the effect of reishi mushrooms on ovarian cancer, scientists discovered that active components of the mushrooms were able to slow down the growth of tumors and cancer cells but also did not harm surrounding healthy cells and tissues. The idea of killing off cancer cells while protecting healthy ones remains a constant challenge for conventional cancer treatment.

Supports cancer cell death

Cells of all kinds or programmed to die, a process known as apotosis; the problem with cancer cells, however, is that they do not undergo this death and keep reproducing endlessly, forming tumors and spreading to other parts of the body. However, extract of reishi mushrooms have been shown to induce apotosis in cancer cells to help stop their spread.

So here, in a nutshell, is a summary of the many health benefits that reishi mushrooms bring to the table. Because of these benefits, reishi mushrooms not just are good at combating cancer but truly can bring improvements to nearly all aspects of general health.

Coach Melvin's Honey-Peach Reishi Power Shake

Take one whole organic peach, several slices of reishi mushroom, a tablespoon of organic honey, blend together in a blender for 10 to 20 seconds.

Cordyceps

Cordyceps originated in Tibet and have long been known as a rare and exotic medicinal mushroom.

Health Benefits:

Cordyceps are used to improve energy levels when recovering from sickness and as a remedy for fatigue and weakness. They contain all 18 essential amino acids along with numerous vitamins and even protein. They are also used to improve respiratory function, heart function, kidney disease and immune function.

People of North Sikkim in India take cordyceps with a cup of milk to increase their sexual desire. Several studies point to cordyceps as being beneficial to testosterone levels.

Antioxidant and antiviral properties: Studies have shown cordyceps as a good free radical scavenger. In a group of studies done in Japan, cordyceps proved to aid in preventing hepatitis C virus, a virus that results in chronic liver disease.

In a study with 50 lung cancer patients, researchers found that taking cordyceps along with chemotherapy reduced tumor sizes by 46%.

How to eat them:

Cordyceps can be eaten whole or cooked with any meal. They can be also taken in tea, as a capsule, powder or tincture.

Turkey Tail (The chewing gum mushroom)

Also known as "cloud mushroom" turkey tail is a colorful mushroom that grows in maroon, blue and green. In Asian culture, this mushroom's curving cloud-like shapes symbolize longevity and health, spiritual attunement and infinity.

Health Benefits:

Turkey tail is used to treat infections, chronic fatigue, pain, to combat respiratory ailments, poor digestion, urinary infections, liver ailments, etc.

Antiviral and antioxidant properties: Eating turkey tail stimulates natural killer cells in the body, which then find virally-infected cells and destroys them. These antiviral compounds are especially good at killing HPC and hepatitis C viruses, which cause cervical and liver cancers. Turkey tail and other medicinal mushrooms are believed to lessen the odds of getting cancer because they beat cancer-causing viruses to the punch. Who knew mushrooms were such powerhouses?

Turkey tail has an incredible influence on the immune system. Ending in 2011, the National Institute of Health funded a $2 million clinical study to find out the effects of turkey tail on the immune system, specifically in women with breast cancer. The polysaccharide complex PSP in turkey tail proved to significantly enhance immune system function in 70-90% of cancer patients.

How to eat them:

Turkey tail can be used as a tincture, extract, in tea, **or even chewed like gum**.

Chapter 17 – Three Super Food Substances:

There are three natural substances in particular that have attracted much enthusiasm from many health-conscious people: one is a nutritional supplement—a superfood. One is a mineral, and the other is a tree. Unfortunately, far too many people are still "in the dark" of just how health-saving these substances are. What am I alluding to? They are OptiMSM, Nahcolite (baking soda), and the Moringa Tree. It is this author's hope that the information compiled here will prompt you to action as well as save you potentially hundreds, if not thousands, of dollars annually:

1. **MSM (methylsulfonylmethane)**, a nutritional supplement already established as a safe, natural, and effective solution for many types of pain and inflammatory conditions,
2. **Nahcolite** from which baking soda is derived,
3. **Moringa Tree (Tree of Life)**

Thousands of people worldwide have benefitted from these powerful organic substances. But this information needs to be disimminated widely so that millions will be privy to this and have it readily available.

Before explaining further about these powerhouses, briefly

The most fantastic thing about MSM, however, is that it is **nontoxic**! There is enough factual evidence that MSM can be taken for chronic, severe, and long-term conditions, and that the medical community should take it seriously. But THEY WON'T because there is not enough profit in it for them. Barring that, each patient is an individual and tends to respond differently to the same drug or supplement., but you will learn that MSM is safe and is helping many people.

MSM is often so effective for pain relief that doctors would be able to lower the dosage of medication they prescribe for their patients. Sometimes they are even able to discontinue the medication. The end result is relief along with fewer or no side effects that are frequently caused by prescriptive pain medications. MSM provides organic, biologically active sulfur—a sorely neglected mineral nutrient. Sulfur has a long tradition of healing and throughout history physicians have prescribed miner hot springs rich in sulfur to their infirm patients.

Then, there's baking soda which hardly anyone uses to it fullest potential, if even at all. In fact, it is a very sad commentary that the world's population is not privy to the numerous uses of this highly beneficial and effective mineral.

Now, take note of what type of conditions MSM can safely relieve, with none of the troubling side effects frequently caused by toxic prescriptive pain medications:

- Degenerative arthritis
- Chronic muscle and back pain
- Chronic headache
- Fibromyalgia
- Tendinitis and bursitis
- Carpal tunnel syndrome
- TMJ
- Dental pain
- Post-traumatic pain and inflammation
- Heartburn and hyperacidity

- Allegeries

- Athletic (sports) injuries

The majority of people when confronted with any of the above injuries or illnesses head straight to their doctor of whom is supposed to be a professional the public should be able to put their trust in, as they are sworn to operate under the principle of "Do no harm." Alas, the majority of allopathic (MDs) doctors are mere puppets of the multibillion dollar pharmaceutical industry. Although doctors already get paid a handsome salary, they still cannot resist the allure of the perpetual cash flow generated by the prescriptions they are so quick to write. The thing that concerns me is that they, for the most part, rely on medications that have significant toxicity and create adverse side effects.

OptiMSM

Explore MSM health benefits

Joint Health   Skin Health   Sports Nutrition   Healthy Aging   General Health

OptiMSM–The World's Purest MSM Is Methyl Sulfonyl Methane, a nutritional *organic* form of sulfur. It is a natural occurring vital nutrient, which is lost through the manufacturing and processing of our food supply. OptiMSM is not a drug, herb or stimulant. It is **completely safe, odorless**, and **non-toxic**. It has been tested and proven to provide relief from many ailments. It is intended as a food supplement only. It is not a medicine or a drug. Studies have shown that it:

- Detoxifies the body
- Allows better absorption of nutrients from food
- Increases circulation
- Reduces inflammation
- Makes hair and nails grow faster
- Relief from allergies through scavenging free radicals
- Reduces lactic acid build-up (less muscle soreness and cramping after exercise
- Relieves chronic fatigue and much more

OptiMSM works better with vitamin C...Take with orange juice (fresh is best) or take with vitamin C supplements; it helps the body to better heal itself! Our bodies make new cells every day of our lives. It is important that our glands put out the right hormones and enzymes to regulate and keep our bodies healthy. Without the proper amount of sulfur (MSM) in our system our bodies cannot produce good healthy cells. We can get this essential nutritional sulfur from some of our foods, but we lose most of this absolutely important mineral by heating, drying, and processing our food. **When your system is deficient in MSM your body cannot make enough good cells to overcome the effects of the bad cells.** We are then subject to various illnesses, aches, pains, and allergies until we correct the problem with good healthy cells.

The body is fully capable of healing itself if it can get the proper nourishment. We all need a little extra OptiMSM each day for good health! The body uses up 1/8 teaspoon of MSM each day during resting time alone. Active or ailing bodies need much more.

> — From The Journal of the New York Academy of Sciences
> Ed. Note: If we all ate nothing but organic raw food every day, we wouldn't need MSM, but this is not the case. Isn't it interesting that when people (and animals) want to get well they go on mono diets, such as grass (animals) wheat grass, aloe vera, other herbs, fresh grape, apple, lemon, or carrot juice? Some of the most spectacular cancer cures have come about in this manner.

Do not confuse organic mineral sulfur from MSM with sulfa-based drugs, sulfites, or sulfates. Sulfa-based drugs (sulfonamide) are a group of large compounds known to cause allergic reactions. Sulfa drugs include erythromycin, sulfisoxazole, sulfamethoxazole, and sulfasalazine. These are drugs composed of many elements creating large chain molecules which are used as antibiotics. It is highly unlikely that anyone would be allergic to MSM or sulfur, a naturally occurring substance in the body.

Sulfites are preservatives, antioxidants and browning agents used in foods. Ingestion of these is associated with adverse reactions such as asthma attacks, nausea, and diarrhea. There are six sulfiting agents currently used: Sodium dioxide, sodium sulfite, sodium and potassium bisulfite, sodium and potassium metasulfite. Sulfates are a salt of sulfuric acid. Sulfuric Acid is a heavy, corrosive, oily acid used in making fertilizers, chemicals and petroleum products.

> MSM is rated as one of the least toxic substances in biology, similar in toxicity to water. If you take more MSM than you need, it simply passes through the body and is excreted in the urine. MSM simply **CANNOT** hurt you.

> MSM has been tested as a food ingredient by Dr. Stanley Jacob without any reports of allergic reaction. An unpublished Oregon Health Sciences University study of the long-term toxicity of MSM over six months showed no toxic effects. More than 12,000 patients have been treated with MSM at levels above two grams daily with no serious toxicity.

Dr. Jacob reports he personally takes 30 grams of MSM per day, and has done so for twenty years. He reports he has not had a cold or the flu since he began this regimen, which he had previously experienced once or twice every year.

> Ed. Note: Race horse trainers use a combination of high powered food supplements, B vitamins and MSM for top performance. MSM is not a stimulant, but allegorically speaking, can be compared to taking all your billions of cells to the car wash for a good cleaning.

As children, the cell membranes that protect our cells are permeable and continually washed by inter- cellular fluids. As we grow older and are exposed to dangerous pollutants, the cell walls become thick. In other words, they go into a defensive mode to keep out the bad guys. However, these less permeable walls allow a slow and deadly buildup of toxic material. MSM makes tissue elastic again and helps to build collagen. With increased permeability, the toxins begin to be washed out of the cells as they were when we were young. With less toxins for our body to deal with we immediately feel more energetic and youthful. Energy that was formerly directed toward detoxification can now be directed toward healing whatever ails us.

Some people who dive into MSM wholeheartedly may experience a toxic headache as the body eliminates into the bloodstream old toxic matter that the cells have been retaining for years. I feel good taking two tablespoons a day, but considering the toxic headache I experienced for a day and a half, would suggest that beginners use a teaspoon twice a day until they clear out a reasonable amount of toxins. Remember, MSM doesn't cause headaches any more than fasting does, it is simply an agent that facilitates the release of accumulated poisons.

Professional athletes work up to using 3 to 4 tablespoons after an especially intense workout to avoid sore muscles the next day. If a normal person were to consume this much MSM they would probably experience an uncomfortable level of detoxification. As with other herbs and health catalysts, it is important to use wisdom and judgment.

I would suggest a teaspoon in the morning and another before five in the evening. Taken too late in the evening, the extra energy one feels can have them up busily doing things when they should be sleeping.

One of the most profound books one can read for the most indepth information and explanation about MSM, is The Miracle of MSM: The Natural Solution For Pain, by Stanley W. Jaccob, M.D., Ronald M. Lawrence, M.D., Ph.D., and Martin Zucker.

Nahcolite (Baking Soda)

Pure sodium bicarbonate is derived from Nahcolite, a naturally occuring mineral already existing in nature. It is found underground or above ground wherever you will find naturally occurring sodium bicarbonate. In North America the Piceance creek basin contains the largest known mines of Nahcolite. This North America Nahcolite mine supplies a large number of the population with the sodium bicarbonate they use for animal feed, and human food. In biblical times the Egyptians used it for cleaning and sanitizing.

The process used to mine Nahcolite is a very simple process of adding hot water to the Nahcolite beds. This causes the Nahcolite to dissolve and can be further extracted as sodium bicarbonate crystals. The crystals begin to form as the hot solution begins to cool.

So, for starters, did you know you can snuff out a small fire with baking soda? And, what about your drains; how many times have you used a plunger or purchased expensive drain cleaners for unclogging? Listed below are scores of ways to use this miracle mineral. However, since it is such an oft-ocurring problem, here's a money-saving solution to any potential drain-clogging problems:

Two items needed:

- a small cloth or drain stopper to temporarily seal the drain, and
- a tea kettle or small pot

Ingredients needed:

- - a box of baking soda
- - 1/2 cup vinegar
- - 1 quart water

Directions

Remove any water remaining in the sink and wait until there is no water left in the drain.

Use approximately half the box of baking soda to pour into the drain.

Having your small cloth or stopper ready, pour 1/2 cup of vinegar down the drain.

Immediately plug the drain with your cloth or stopper because the interaction of the vinegar and baking soda will be powerful enough to cause an eruption. The good thing about it is that if perhaps you are splashed, unlike like toxic drain cleaners, you will not be harmed or burned. Let the baking soda/vinegar remain in the drain for 30 minutes. Then, pour boiling water down the drain. Problem solved!

Fights Cancer

Baking soda has been a natural, safe, effective and affordable alternative to using harsh chemicals. It can be used in hundreds of different ways.

But it is little known that baking soda is also an essential medicine, which no emergency room or intensive care ward would be caught without. This section gives just a synopsis of the knowledge and scope of sodium bicarbonates use in medicine.

That cheap little box sitting on your grocer's shelf---although it gets many sales---has been long ignored by the majority of consumers. Little do they know what a super power this box of white powder is. And, when mixed with lemons, the healing and preventive effect is totally astounding.

For example, together lemon and baking soda help to fight cancerous cells or diseases in the body while helping to increase the body's ability to clean itself up of what may be causing the diseases in the first place. Having lemon as a part of your diet is certainly healthy and taking this combination as a detox can also be helpful even if you don't have an illness.

One method found for introducing this into your body as a drink is to mix 1/2 teaspoon of baking soda into 250ml of water with about 1 half of a lemon. There are, however, more recipes that might work for you. I have personally taken this mixture if I ever had stomach issues or was feeling like I might be getting sick. It has been very successful each time I've used it. Of course, you should always do your own research and, if you happen to have a regular doctor who is closed-minded, you should opt for a second medical opinion from an "alternative" health professional if you wish. The "alternative" health professional I am speaking of is one that is well-versed in Traditional Chinese Medicine and herbs, or a practitioner of medical Qigong with decades of experience treating patients, like the highly qualified individuals at the end of this book.

Now here's a list of all the things Baking Soda can powerfully do in the most cost-effective way:

Personal Care

1. Make Toothpaste

A paste made from baking soda and a 3 percent hydrogen peroxide solution can be used as an alternative to commercial non-fluoride toothpastes. (Or here's a formula for a minty version.) You can also just dip your toothbrush with toothpaste into baking soda for an extra boost.

2. Freshens Your Mouth

Put one teaspoon in half a glass of water, swish, spit and rinse. Odors are neutralized, not just covered up.

3. Soak Oral Appliance

Soak oral appliances, like retainers, mouthpieces and dentures, in a solution of 2 teaspoons baking soda dissolved in a glass or small bowl of warm water. The baking soda loosens food particles and neutralizes odors to keep appliances fresh. You can also brush appliances clean using baking soda.

4. Use as a Facial Scrub and Body Exfoliant

Give yourself an invigorating facial and body scrub. Make a paste of 3 parts baking soda to 1 part water. Rub in a gentle circular motion to exfoliate the skin. Rinse clean. This is gentle enough for daily use. (For a stronger exfoliant, try one of these great 5 Homemade Sugar Scrubs.)

5. Skip Harsh Deodorant

Pat baking soda onto your underarms to neutralize body odor.

6. Use as an Antacid

Baking soda is a safe and effective antacid to relieve heartburn, sour stomach and/or acid indigestion. Refer to baking soda package for instructions.

7. Treat Insect Bites & Itchy Skin

For insect bites, make a paste out of baking soda and water, and apply as a salve onto affected skin. To ease the itch, shake some baking soda into your hand and rub it into damp skin after bath or shower. For specific tips on bee stings, see Bee Stings: Prevention and Treatment.

8. Make a Hand Cleanser and Softener

Skip harsh soaps and gently scrub away ground-in dirt and neutralize odors on hands with a paste of 3 parts baking soda to 1 part water, or 3 parts baking soda to gentle liquid hand soap. Then rinse clean. For example, 3/4 cup of baking soda mixed in 1/4 pure water.

9. Help Your Hair

Vinegar is amazing for your hair, but baking soda has its place in the shower too. Sprinkle a small amount of baking soda into your palm along with your favorite shampoo. Shampoo as usual and rinse thoroughly–baking soda helps remove the residue that styling products leave behind so your hair is cleaner and more manageable.

10. Clean Brushes and Combs

For lustrous hair with more shine, keep brushes and combs clean. Remove natural oil build-up and hair product residue by soaking combs and brushes in a solution of 1 teaspoon of baking soda in a small basin of warm water. Rinse and allow to dry.

11. Make a Bath Soak

Add 1/2 cup of baking soda to your bath to neutralize acids on the skin and help wash away oil and perspiration, it also makes your skin feel very soft. Epsom salts are pretty miraculous for the bath too; read about the health benefits of epsom salt baths.

12. Soothe Your Feet

Dissolve 3 tablespoons of baking soda in a tub of warm water and soak feet. Gently scrub. You can also make a spa soak for your feet.

Cleaning

13. Make a Surface Soft Scrub

For safe, effective cleaning of bathroom tubs, tile and sinks—even fiberglass and glossy tiles—sprinkle baking soda lightly on a clean damp sponge and scrub as usual. Rinse thoroughly and wipe dry. For extra cleaning power, make a paste with baking soda, course salt and liquid dish soap—let it sit then scour off.

14. Handwash Dishes and Pots & Pans

Add 2 heaping tablespoons baking soda (along with your regular dish detergent) to the dish water to help cut grease and foods left on dishes, pots and pans. For cooked-on foods, let them soak in the baking soda and detergent with water first, then use dry baking soda on a clean damp sponge or cloth as a scratchless scouring powder. Using a dishwasher? Try these energy saving tips.

15. Freshen Sponges

Soak stale-smelling sponges in a strong baking soda solution to get rid of the mess (4 tablespoons of baking soda dissolved in 1 quart of warm water). For more thorough disinfecting, use the microwave.

16. Clean the Microwave

Baking soda on a clean damp sponge cleans gently inside and outside the microwave and never leaves a harsh chemical smell. Rinse well with water.

17. Polish Silver Flatware

Use a baking soda paste made with 3 parts baking soda to 1 part water. Rub onto the silver with a clean cloth or sponge. Rinse thoroughly and dry for shining sterling and silver-plate serving pieces.

18. Clean Coffee and Tea Pots

Remove coffee and tea stains and eliminate bitter off-tastes by washing mugs and coffee makers in a solution of 1/4 cup baking soda in 1 quart of warm water. For stubborn stains, try soaking overnight in the baking soda solution and detergent or scrubbing with baking soda on a clean damp sponge.19. **Clean the Oven**

Sprinkle baking soda onto the bottom of the oven. Spray with water to dampen the baking soda. Let sit overnight. In the morning, scrub, scoop the baking soda and grime out with a sponge, or vacuum, and rinse.

20. Clean Floors

Remove dirt and grime (without unwanted scratch marks) from no wax and tile floors using 1/2 cup baking soda in a bucket of warm water–mop and rinse clean for a sparkling floor. For scuff marks, use baking soda on a clean damp sponge, then rinse. Read Natural Floor Cleaning for more tips on avoiding toxic floor cleaners.

21. Clean Furniture

You can make a homemade lemon furniture polish, or you can clean and remove marks (even crayon) from walls and painted furniture by applying baking soda to a damp sponge and rubbing lightly. Wipe off with a clean, dry cloth.

22. Clean Shower Curtains

Clean and deodorize your vinyl shower curtain by sprinkling baking soda directly on a clean damp sponge or brush. Scrub the shower curtain and rinse clean. Hang it up to dry.

23. Boost Your Liquid Laundry Detergent

Give your laundry a boost by adding 1/2 cup of baking soda to your laundry to make liquid detergent work harder. A better balance of pH in the wash gets clothes cleaner, fresher and brighter.

24. **Gently Clean Baby Clothes**

Baby skin requires the most gentle of cleansers, which are increasingly available, but odor and stain fighters are often harsh. For tough stains add 1/2 cup of baking soda to your liquid laundry detergent, or a 1/2 cup in the rinse cycle for deodorization.

25. **Clean Cloth Diapers**

Dissolve 1/2 cup of baking soda in 2 quarts of water and soak diapers thoroughly.

26. **Clean and Freshen Sports Gear**

Use a baking soda solution (4 tablespoons baking soda in 1 quart warm water) to clean and deodorize smelly sports equipment. Sprinkle baking soda into golf bags and gym bags to deodorize, clean golf irons (without scratching them!) with a baking soda paste (3 parts baking soda to 1 part water) and a brush. Rinse thoroughly.

27. **Remove Oil and Grease Stains**

Use baking soda to clean up light-duty oil and grease spills on your garage floor or in your driveway. Sprinkle baking soda on the spot and scrub with a wet brush.

28. **Clean Batteries**

Baking soda can be used to neutralize battery acid corrosion on cars, mowers, etc. because its a mild alkali. Be sure to disconnect the battery terminals before cleaning. Make a paste of 3 parts baking soda to 1 part water, apply with a damp cloth to scrub corrosion from the battery terminal. After cleaning and re-connecting the terminals, wipe them with petroleum jelly to prevent future corrosion. Please be careful when working around a battery–they contain a strong acid.

29. **Clean Cars**

Use baking soda to clean your car lights, chrome, windows, tires, vinyl seats and floor mats without worrying about unwanted scratch marks. Use a baking soda solution of 1/4 cup baking soda in 1 quart of warm water. Apply with a sponge or soft cloth to remove road grime, tree sap, bugs and tar. For stubborn stains, use baking soda sprinkled on a damp sponge or soft brush

Deodorizing

30. Deodorize Your Refrigerator

Place an open box in the back of the fridge to neutralize odors.

31. Deodorize the Cutting Board

Sprinkle the cutting board with baking soda, scrub, rinse. For how to more thoroughly clean your cutting board, see How To Clean Your Cutting Boards.

32. Deodorize Trashcans

Sprinkle baking soda on the bottom of your trashcan to keep stinky trash smells at bay.

33. Deodorize Recyclables

Sprinkle baking soda on top as you add to the container. Also, clean your recyclable container periodically by sprinkling baking soda on a damp sponge. Wipe clean and rinse. Learn about how to recycle everything.

34. Deodorize Drains

To deodorize your sink and tub drains, and keep lingering odors from resurfacing, pour 1/2 cup of baking soda down the drain while running warm tap water–it will neutralize both acid and basic odors for a fresh drain. (This a good way to dispose of baking soda that is being retired from your refrigerator.) Do you know what you're not supposed to put down your drains?

35. Deodorize and Clean Dishwashers

Use baking soda to deodorize before you run the dishwasher and then as a gentle cleanser in the wash cycle.

36. Deodorize Garbage Disposals

To deodorize your disposal, and keep lingering odors from resurfacing, pour baking soda down the drain while running warm tap water. Baking soda will neutralize both acid and basic odors for a fresh drain.

37. Deodorize Lunch Boxes

Between uses, place a spill-proof box of baking soda in everyone's lunch box to absorb lingering odors. Read bout safe lunch boxes here.

38. Remove Odor From Carpets

Liberally sprinkle baking soda on the carpet. Let set overnight, or as long as possible (the longer it sets the better it works). Sweep up the larger amounts of baking soda, and vacuum up the rest. (Note that your vacuum cleaner bag will get full and heavy.)

39. Remove Odor From Vacuum Cleaners

By using the method above for carpets, you will also deodorize your vacuum cleaner.

40. Freshen Closets

Place a box on the shelf to keep the closet smelling fresh.

41. Deodorizing Cars

Odors settle into car upholstery and carpet, so each time you step in and sit down, they are released into the air all over again. Eliminate these odors by sprinkling baking soda directly on fabric car seats and carpets. Wait 15 minutes (or longer for strong odors) and vacuum up the baking soda.

42. Deodorize the Cat Box

Cover the bottom of the pan with baking soda, then fill as usual with litter. To freshen between changes, sprinkle baking soda on top of the litter after a thorough cleaning. You can also use green tea for this purpose!

43. Deodorize Pet Bedding

Eliminate odors from your pets bedding by sprinkling liberally with baking soda, wait 15 minutes (or longer for stronger odors), then vacuum up.

44. Deodorize Sneakers

Keep odors from spreading in smelly sneakers by shaking baking soda into them when not in use. Shake out before wearing. When they're no longer wearable, make sure to donate your old sneakers.

45. Freshen Linens

Add 1/2 cup of baking soda to the rinse cycle for fresher sheets and towels.

46. Deodorize Your Wash

Gym clothes of other odoriferous clothing can be neutralized with a 1/2 cup of baking soda in the rinse cycle.

47. Freshen Stuffed Animals

Keep favorite cuddly toys fresh with baking soda. Sprinkle baking soda on and let it sit for 15 minutes before brushing off.

Miscellaneous

48. Camping Cure-all

Baking soda is a must-have for your next camping trip. Its a dish washer, pot scrubber, hand cleanser, deodorant, toothpaste, fire extinguisher and many other uses.

49. Extinguish Fires

Baking soda can help in the initial handling of minor grease or electrical kitchen fires, because when baking soda is heated, it gives off carbon dioxide, which helps to smother the flames. For small cooking fires (frying pans, broilers, ovens, grills), turn off the gas or electricity if you can safely do so. Stand back and throw handfuls of baking soda at the base of the flame to help put out the fire—and call the Fire Department just to be safe. (And, you should have a fire extinguisher on hand anyway, here's why.

50. Septic Care

Regular use of baking soda in your drains can help keep your septic system flowing freely. One cup of baking soda per week will help maintain a favorable pH in your septic tank.

51. Fruit and Vegetable Scrub

Baking soda is the food-safe way to clean dirt and residue off fresh fruit and vegetables. Just sprinkle a little on a clean damp sponge, scrub and rinse.

SOURCE: http://www.care2.com/greenliving/51-fantastic-uses-for-baking-soda.html#ixzz3HzAJXfii

Now, armed with this info you should be able to save hundreds or thousands or more dollars a year just by using baking soda for the above tasks instead of myriad expensive store products—some of which may be toxic to small children—you have purchased over the years. **PLUS**, you can save on visits to the doctor or dentist. And, that's money in the hand.

MORINGA TREE (Moringa oleifera)

Moringa was highly valued in the ancient world. The Romans, Greeks and Egyptians extracted edible oil from the seeds and used it for perfume and skin lotion.

Claims of Traditional Medicine. For centuries, people in many countries have used Moringa leaves as traditional medicine for common ailments.

During the 19th century, plantations of Moringa in the West Indies exported the oil to Europe for perfumes and lubricants for machinery. People in the Indian sub-continent have long used Moringa pods for food. The edible leaves are eaten throughout West Africa and in parts of Asia.

The leaves of this tree are worthy of special attention. Traditional medicine in several countries has used these leaves to cure a host of diseases. Clinical studies are suggesting that traditional medicine has been on the right track.

Nutritional analyses show that the leaves are very high in protein and contain all of the essential amino acids, including two amino acids that are especially important for children's diets. This is most uncommon in a plant food.

Moringa is a fast-growing, drought-resistant tree that grows even in marginal soils and with very little care.

Every part of the Moringa tree is said to have beneficial properties that can serve humanity. People in societies around the world have made use of these properties.

One of the most remarkably useful trees is one being cultivated heavily for use in the Sudan. The Food and Agriculture Organization of the United Nations said that village women had successfully used the tree Moringa oleifera (pictured at top) to cleanse the highly turbid water of the River Nile. After trying other moringa species in Egypt, Namibia, Somalia, and Kenya, they too have shown properties that clarify water quickly.

Bottles of dirty and clean water When moringa seeds are crushed and poured into a pot or bottle of dirty water, the water turns transparent within seconds. The seeds' anti-bacterial properties can turn low, medium, and high turbidity waters into tap-water quality in an hour or two.

Studies on the effectiveness of moringa seeds for treating water have been done since the 1970s, and have consistently shown that moringa is especially effective in removing suspended particles from water with medium to high levels of turbidity (muddiness or dirtiness).

In water with high turbidity, a litre of water needs only one of the horseradish-smelling seeds for effective treatment. In low turbity, one seed may do 4 litres. When the water is boiled, this increases its nutritional effectiveness by making inactive a nutrition-inhibiting protein (lectin).

Case Study: Moringa Leaf Powder Treating Malnutrition In 1997-98, Alternative Action for African Development (AGADA) and Church World Service tested the ability of Moringa leaf powder to prevent or cure malnutrition in pregnant or breast-feeding women and their children in southwestern Senegal.5, 19 Malnutrition was a major problem in this area, with more than 600 malnourished infants treated every year. During the test, doctors, nurses, and midwives were trained in preparing and using Moringa leaf powder for treating malnutrition. Village women were also trained in the preparation and use of Moringa leaf powder in foods. This test found the following effects to be common among subjects taking Moringa leaf powder:

- Children maintained or increased their weight and improved overall health.
- Pregnant women recovered from anemia and had babies with higher birth weights.
- Breast-feeding women increased their production of milk.

The leaves are inexpensive and are used in soups, and with meat, chicken and vegetable dishes. The leaves are somewhat like spinach in both looks and nutritional value. Fresh leaves have 4 times the calcium of milk, 7 times the vitamin C in oranges, and 4 times the vitamin A in carrots. They are used in tea, soup, and porridge.

Moringa's bark, roots, fruit, flowers, leaves, seeds (photo at right) and gum are used as an antiseptic and in medicines to treat rheumatism, bites and other ailments. The seed pod has been used to desalinate sea water.

The bark and roots are used as a spice and in soap; seed oil is used in cooking, machine lubrication, and cosmetics; the wood is used for fences and firewood.

Today billions of people on our planet suffer from malnutrition. Their pain and suffering cannot even be imagined. It is a chronic and urgent problem that will not go away easily. To address this problem we will need every tool possible at our command, and perhaps Moringa can play a role. If you can assist in initiating further studies please contact: www.Moringa@TreesForLife.org

Although there have been references to the Moringa Oleifera tree that go back a couple thousand years, and the World Health Organization has been studying and using the plant for the last forty years as a low cost health enhancer in the poorest countries around the world, this little known tree has just recently been making headlines in the Western World. Moringa translates to mean "miracle" and the Moringa tree truly is nature's miracle. Packed with over 90 nutrients and 46 antioxidants, this plant is being hailed by nutritionists as the "nutritional dynamite of the century."

The Highest Nutritional Content of Any Plant

Ideal for helping our bodies maintain optimum health, Moringa leaves have been traditionally used to combat numerous conditions. Many people taking Moringa have reported improvements in their skin, digestion, eyesight, mental clarity, and overall well-being, plus a reduction in symptoms associated with fatigue, arthritic-like conditions, and aging, to name a few. Some studies also show that Moringa is effective in maintaining healthy blood pressure levels, alleviating pains caused by migraines or headaches, and helping the immune system.

Moringa Oilfiera Leaves have been used traditionally to:

- Help Regulate a Healthy Metabolism
- Boost the Body's Natural Defenses
- Promote Healthy Cell Structure
- Support Healthy Cholesterol Levels
- Promote Healthy Skin
- Assist Weight Control and Digestion
- Increase Energy Levels
- Support Healthy Blood Sugar Levels
- Promote a Healthy Circulatory System
- Help Detoxify the Body

- Alleviating Headaches
- Help Prevent Hair Loss

Testimonies:

"Although few people have ever heard of it today, Moringa could soon become one of the world's most valuable plants, at least in humanitarian terms."

- Noel Vietmeyer, US National Academy of Sciences, Washington D.C

"A major advantage to Moringa is the fact that it is a local resource.

This contrasts with many of the ongoing programs designed to fight

malnutrition which depend on imported products and outside

support. …Moringa is a very simple and readily available solution to

the problem of malnutrition."

- Lowell J. Fuglie, in The Miracle Tree - Moringa oleifera: Natural Nutrition for the Tropics

" Moringa shows great promise as a tool to help overcome some of

the most severe problems in the developing world—malnutrition,

deforestation, impure water and poverty. The tree does best in the

dry regions where these problems are worst."

- Andrew Young, former Atlanta Mayor and United Nations Ambassador

Special Note of Interest

This info credited to Mike Adams*

There is a curious tendency in conventional medicine to label a set of symptoms as a disease. For example, I recently spotted a poster touting a new drug for osteoporosis. It was written by a drug company and it said this: "Osteoporosis is a disease that causes weak and fragile bones." The poster went on to say that you need a particular drug to counteract this "disease."

Yet the language is all backward. Osteoporosis is not a disease that causes weak bones. Osteoporosis is the name given to a diagnosis of weak bones. In other words, the weak bones happened first, and then the diagnosis followed.

Another drug company defines osteoporosis as "the disease that causes bones to become thinner." Again, the cause and effect are reversed. And that's how drug companies want people to think about diseases and symptoms: First you "get" the disease, then you are "diagnosed" just in time to take an expensive new drug for the rest of your life.

But it's all hogwash. There is no such disease as osteoporosis. It's just a name for a pattern of symptoms that indicate you've let your bones get fragile. And to treat it, western doctors will give you prescriptions for drugs that claim to make your bones less brittle.

We should really call it Brittle Bones Disease, and describe the treatment in plain language - exercise, vitamin D, mineral supplements with calcium and strontium, natural sunlight, and the avoidance of substances like soft drinks, white flour, and added sugars, which strip away bone mass.

Diabetes is another condition given a complex name that puts its solution out of reach of the average patient. Type 2 diabetes isn't technically a disease. It's just a natural metabolic side effect of consuming refined carbohydrates and added sugars in large quantities without engaging in regular physical exercise.

The name "diabetes" is meaningless to the average person. It should be called Excessive Sugar Disease. If it were called Excessive Sugar Disease, the solution to it would be rather apparent.

Cancer is another disease named after its symptom. To this day, most doctors and patients still believe that cancer is a physical thing: a tumor. In reality, a tumor is only a side effect of cancer, not its cause. A tumor is simply a physical manifestation of a cancer pattern that is expressed by the body.

When a person "has cancer," what they really have is a sluggish or suppressed immune system. And that would be a far better name for the disease: Suppressed Immune System Disorder.

If cancer were actually called that, it would seem ridiculous to try to cure it by cutting out tumors and destroying the immune system with chemotherapy. These are the two most popular treatments for cancer, and they do nothing to support the patient's immune system or prevent future occurrences. That's exactly why most people who undergo chemotherapy or the removal of tumors end up with yet more cancer down the road.

The cure for cancer already exists, and it's found in every human body. Your body kills cancer cells as a routine daily task, and it has done it thousands of times in your lifetime.

All we have to do is stop poisoning our bodies with cancer-causing chemicals and start feeding ourselves the materials our bodies need to beat chronic disease. Instead of searching for new technological cures, our money and time would be better spent making people aware of the existing cures and prevention strategies available right now.

Here's another example: high cholesterol. Conventional medicine says that high cholesterol is caused by a chemical imbalance in the liver, the organ that produces cholesterol. Thus the treatment is drugs (statin drugs) that inhibit the liver's production of cholesterol. Upon taking these drugs, the high cholesterol (the "disease") is regulated.

But the fatal flaw in this approach is once again evident: The symptom is not the cause of the disease. There is another cause, one that is routinely ignored by conventional medicine, doctors, drug companies, and even patients. The root cause of high cholesterol is primarily dietary. A person who eats foods that are high in saturated fats and hydrogenated oils will inevitably produce more bad cholesterol. It's simple cause and effect, not some bizarre behavior by the liver.

"There's a great deal of ego invested in the medical community, and they sure don't want to make health sound attainable to the average person."

Conclusion

In our fast-paced society, so many people believe you must jump, dive, roll, tumble, bounce or develop a muscular body frame by perpetually lifting weights in order to be fit, in shape, or get excellent results from an exercise program. Exercise does not have to be done at a mind-warping pace to achieve the desired results of a fit and healthy body. Indeed, the so-called "no pain, no gain" mentality mostly does more harm than good, especially if you are a weekend warrior—a person who tries to do it all on weekend bouts instead of on a consistent three-or-four-days-a-week cycle.

The Book on Amazing, Internal STRESS *Release* was written for people who want to live without stress, get in shape, and be totally healthy. It contains the 10 basic, but vital steps you need to achieve all of these. If you feel any pain or discomfort while you are performing any of the 10 steps within the pages of this book, take measures to avoid or alleviate this discomfort. These adaptations might include any or all of the following:

- do fewer repetitions,

- slow down,

- ease up or

- discontinue until the issue is corrected

It is important to take the above precaution(s) until you have ascertained either what is causing the pain or located the source of the pain and have addressed it, ensuring that continuing with the 10 Steps will not cause further pain.

Again, in performing any of the *Steps*, always back off a little until you feel no strain, discomfort, or pain. Pain is our body's way of indicating that something is wrong. It lets you know that, if you continue, you risk potentially adverse effects on your health.

Done a minimum of three times a week, the practices shown within this book will help limber your body over a period of time—weeks or months, depending on your body structure and natural flexibility—and help you maintain moderately good health.

Becoming well-versed in all included in *The Book on Internal* STRESS *Release* gives you flexibility of movement and reservoirs of energy. It also allows you to easily understand and practice movements of the popular Tai Chi you see almost everywhere these days.

About the Author

Coach Melvin, an internationally-known, award-winning author, is Chief Instructor at Heaven's Palm Boxing Association (a Los Angeles-based martial arts school, which is a subsidiary of Kanda Equity Holdings, LLC, the Coach's asset management firm he oversees), where he teaches Qigong meditation, as well as the internal martial arts, Taijiquan (Tai Chi Chuan) and Baguazhang. As an entrepreneur, he's a Founder at The ICA Network (a mobile technology company instrumental in bringing the world's businesses out of the Web 2.0 state, changing them to Mobile-friendly, Mobile-optimized, and Responsive-designed powerhouses of the current Web 3.0 where most of the world uses and is connected by mobile devices). He is also Founding Brand Ambassador at Zindigo Inc., (an innovative one-of-a-kind Online social commerce platform that enjoys exclusive representation of world-class fashion designers, bringing the cost of *celebrity* fashions down to a level of affordability by the masses); The Coach has committed his life to helping people become both exceptionally healthy and financially secure.

In this publication, which is a revision of his previous award-winning book, Coach Melvin includes two gifts for the health benefit of the reader: an Online organic and whole-food membership warehouse club similar to one of the leading American membership-only warehouse clubs. However, this membership-only warehouse club allows average people to purchase **individual items** at wholesale prices. The other is the gift of music. Food feeds your body, while music feeds your soul. They work incredibly well together to help you to take more time to address health issues or take part in health-producing activities that vitalizes your livelihood. As for being healthy, the Coach has utilized his own powerfu DAIA Method for many years and, along with Dr. Painter's method, and Dr. Totton's method, shows you how to take conscious control of your mind and body so you can insulate yourself from debilitating negative energy with internal stress release, thereby producing a balanced mind.

Coach Melvin, and his two colleague's current passion is teaching people just like you how, by being committed to the practices contained within the pages of this publication, to first, raze the negative stress you may have, and second, to prevent it from ever invading the perimeter of your mind/body again. This will dramatically change your life for the better.

You don't have to reinvent the wheel. You just have to follow the "Guaranteed Path to Exceptional Health" found within the pages of his book.

In "The Book on Internal STRESS Release" you'll discover:

- Exactly how to practically melt away negative stress energy like ice melting on a hot surface, so that you'll enjoy the benefit of amazing, internal stress release.
- Why internal stress release is the key that opens the way to perpetual mental and physical rejuvenation.
- A dead-simple way to lock out the negative stress that keeps you from living the life you want
- Why "negative stress" is the lock on the gate that keeps radiant health out…and much, much more

Many practitioners of Qigong incorporate the internal martial arts into their regimen as well as practices of varying forms of Buddhism, Taoism or other esoteric Eastern religions, philosophies, or methods of. However, though Qigong meditation plays a major role in his health regimen, Coach Melvin chooses Christianity, and practices the internal martial arts within the tenets of his faith. He lives by the methods he shares in this book and willingly shares the power of his faith with all who inquire. Within his own practice and meditation the Coach says, "I do not attempt to become one with the universe for I have become one with the *Creator* of the universe."

The Coach is author of best-selling, Defend Yourself: Secrets to Protect Yourself from a Hostile Dog Attack, which was newly released as an ebook under the title, **Secrets Revealed: Protect Yourself From a Hostile Dog Attack**. He also authored, Incredible Stress Relief: The Ice, Water, Gas Method, with E. Claudette Freeman. (www.eclaudetteliterary.com). Currently, however, he is authoring his highly anticipated, historically significant, **Profiles of African-American Tai Chi Masters: Get Powerful Martial Arts Secrets**, featuring twenty of America's top internal martial arts pioneers. Coach Melvin has already flown to various cities around the country interviewing some of these esteemed professionals, one of whom is listed in the **List of Preeminent Qigong / Tai Chi Chuan Masters**. With a few more to interview, his next publication will follow on the heels of this book.

Note: For becoming seriously involved with more training

If you have a strong desire to give copious time towards developing your internal energy to levels higher than the basics taught by Coach Melvin in chapter two, it is strongly suggested you follow the superb intermediate method of Board-Certified pyschologist, Dr. Carl Totton, or immerse yourself in the advance concepts of Dr. John P. Painter.

As shared by my mentor Bruce Frantzis, the following should be considered for novices who want to begin with the basics. However, you should seriously contemplate your course of action and with whom you will study:

The Basics

The basics in the internal arts are exercises that are extremely important. As they are the very fabric upon which all else is built, *much* time should be spent on developing all of your basics. Being grounded in the basics gives you a strong, stable foundation upon which you can begin to build the complex movements of the internal arts. It cannot be emphasized enough how much the basics will enhance and add quality to all of your movements.

Bear in your mind, the more time you spend on strengthening your foundation (basics) now, the less you will need to think about *them* later. Your body will have naturally adapted, become properly aligned and old habits will have dissipated.

The Time - There is a significant time factor involved in the development of the internal arts. One cannot have a "monkey-mind" if progress is to be expected. A monkey-minded person jumps from place to place without staying long enough to significantly develop anything. If one wants instant *gratification*, my suggestion would be to get involved in low level external arts such as karate or judo as those forms of practice are easy to learn and do not require intensive mental concentration. That is also one of the reasons why they are so popular.

Although there is physical movement involved in the internal arts you must make it a point to become aware of the internal process which involves the movement. Becoming aware of your internal components allow you to mentally "feel" the insides of your body. This in turn allows you to actually use your mind to direct (move) energy (chi) within your body to bring about desirable effects. All of this, however, requires the four-letter word, "time." As this is not a rapid-results art, you should endeavor to make it part of your daily routine without giving thought as to when you will be able to direct your chi. Focus your thoughts instead on building a strong, stable foundation, internal body alignment, breathing, relaxation, and being aware of any internal happenings within your body. Practicing with this frame of mind will produce better results as your mind will not be cluttered with thoughts of, "When will I get my next belt?" "When will I be promoted to the next level?"

Repetition (**daily practice**) is the key to success. Here are three rules for reaching your goal:

Rule #1 - Practice

Rule #2 - Practice

Rule #3 - When in doubt, see rule #1

The Practice - Standing Meditation - This is one of the initial stages whereby you begin to develop chi. By standing completely still your mind does not have to worry about doing any physical motions. Therefore, you can *completely* focus on your internal components. Further, by closing your eyes, your mind will not be distracted by external surroundings. This exercise helps you to achieve greater body relaxation both externally and internally.

Stand straight, mouth closed, tongue against the roof of your mouth, chest dropped, shoulders dropped, feet approximately shoulder width apart, belly relaxed, hips tucked under, arms at your sides with palms facing back, knees slightly bent, breathe low into lower abdominal area.

After obtaining the above position, with eyes closed, begin to use just your mind to become aware of sensations within your body. Start at the top of your head and "release" any tension you may notice anywhere: forehead, eyes, ears, cheeks, lips (are they pursed?), teeth (are they clenched?), tongue (is it "pushed against the palate or lightly held there?). From these, continue floating down your body as you become increasingly (meaning over a period of TIME = months) aware of your internal self, releasing tension as you continue downward until you reach your feet. Be advised that to become internally "aware" of the lower portions of the body requires a significant amount of time and cannot be achieved without consistent practice over a couple of years.

Gifts From the Coach

The Book on Internal STRESS Release: Get Powerful Health and Nutritional Secrets, **rewards *you* further with two included gifts. Actually, these gifts establish the validity of this book.**

Gift #1 – *NEVER PAY FULL RETAIL again on healthy, natural and organic food products.* Coach Melvin believes everyone should have access to quality, healthy food. FREE access to 4000+ healthy, natural products up to 50% off, with free delivery to your door - **www.More.sh/Organic-Healthfood**

Ditching junk food and switching to the healthier choice does not have to be a financial pain. In fact, you can actually save both time and money when you choose to ***make*** a handful of simple swaps. It's simple and easy for members on a budget to stay healthy. Whether you're hunting for safe sunscreen, or looking to satisfy your sweet-tooth minus refined sugar, click the link above for the highest-quality non-GMO products you love at the lowest possible prices.

Gift #2 – MUSIC IS AN EXCELLENT STRESS RELEASER - How would you like to learn from a **robot...a song robot**? Watch it in action! Check out this FREE video and software demonstration! **www.More.sh/Computer-SongTutor**

Even if you've never, EVER touched a piano keyboard or synthesizer during your entire lifetime, this FREE presentation shows you how a music robot can teach you anything you ever wanted to know about music. You can actually start playing your favorite songs within minutes with a new revolutionary tool never shared in public...**UNTIL NOW!** Discover secrets even most musicians will never know about playing by ear. Learn any song by understanding one thing: like how to use just 4 chords and a handful of patterns to play any song you want!

Visit the link above to fulfill that life-long dream of learning piano, organ, guitar, *drums*, or any other instruments by ear, without reading sheet music; there's nothing to lose and everything to gain.

SPECIAL INCLUSION: LIST of PREEMINENT QIGONG / TAI CHI CHUAN MASTERS Included below in this publication.

This inclusion features an A-list of highly skilled Qigong and Internal Martial Arts masters. These esteemed professionals—some of them highly qualified MDs, NDs, DOs, O.M.Ds, herbologists, and Ph.Ds, working in medical clinics and hospitals, in addition to their martial prowess, utilize healing methods quite different from your typical medical doctor. Over the years, they have collectively helped hundreds of thousands of individuals with myriad medical issues. Their sought-after medical skills, Qigong, and Internal Martial Arts are a boon to the patient.

Coach Melvin wants you to be mentally and physically healthy, having a life filled with abundance and joy—just like his—because he truly believes that "in the giving is the receiving."

Note: The healing modality of these professionals take into account the mind, body, and soul of the patient, which is a holistic approach to healing. Rather than focusing only on the symptoms of an illness, or separate body parts, they use an integrative system that makes use of a variety of natural healing therapies, the most common being:

Qigong (chee - gung)

Energy Healing

Massage

Acupressure

Reflexology

Nutrition & Diet

Herbology

Homeopathy

Aromatherapy

Sound Healing*

*Music qualifies as "sound healing" because of the pleasant mental benefits derived from listening to it. That is why it is one of the Coach's gifts to you.

List of Preeminent Qigong / Tai Chi Chuan Masters

Featuring Grandmaster Zhou Ting-Jue

http://www.masterzhou.com

Dr. Zhou was featured on numerous television programs, including: "That's Incredible" and "Ripley's Believe It Or Not" www.youtube.com/watch?v=20GnC0F37K8. He was showcased on a season of The History Channel's hit show "Stan Lee's Superhumans," in recognition of his amazing abilities—verified by ample scientific, diagnostic and medical research documentation, for decades.

Dr. Zhou has taught and treated everyone from His Holiness, the Dalai Lama, players of the LA Lakers, to Olympians, celebrities, entertainers, spiritual masters and dignitaries, internationally. Seventy-eight-year-old Grandmaster Zhou Ting-Jue is so highly respected in China, that he has been called a "Treasure of the Nation" and, "The Jewel of China."

His Qi Gong healing treatments have been known to dissolve tumors, heal severe, chronic injuries, as well as successfully treat "incurable" diseases. Because of this and his amazing skills as a medical intuitive, in diagnosing mystery illnesses, people travel the world to be treated by him.

A sample of symptoms and conditions treated:

-- Brain, nerve, neurological or other chronic pain or damage;

-- Chronic injuries and/or illness, including speeding up recovery and healing after surgery and/or chemical injury;

-- Ailments of the eyes, ears, nose, throat and lungs/respiratory organs;

-- Heart, blood and blood vessels diseases;

-- Skin, bone, joint or injury-related illnesses or disorders;

-- Liver, kidneys, gall bladder, pancreas, spleen diseases or illnesses;

-- Tumors, cysts and other growths, including all forms of cancer;

-- Immunological conditions and auto-immunity, immune function or weakness; Lupus, CFS, Fibromyalgia;

--Stomach, digestive tract and intestinal tract malfunctions;

--Emotional challenges, PTSD, ADD/ADHD, Panic/Anxiety, Depression, Insomnia, and

-- Gender-specific issues, including: male and female sexual imbalances such as infertility, impotence, prostate and gynecological issues, including recovery from pregnancy loss or miscarriage;

...and many others.

Listed in alphabetical order.

Alan Lamb

http://www.alanlambwingchun.com

Sifu Alan Lamb is from England, and a Hong Kong trained master of Wing Chun Kung-Fu, and Chi Gung Energy Healing. With over 40 years of teaching experience under his belt, he has taught classes around the World, including the U.S.A, South America, London and Europe. He taught for two years at the Royal National Institute for the Blind, specifically working with a group of blind physical therapist students from all over the World whom resided at the London academy. He also taught one of the top neurologists in Los Angeles, who encouraged him to put together a program for stroke victims. As well as being a published author, Sifu Lamb now focuses on teaching Energy Healing classes and Chi Gung workshops, plus he is also available for motivational speaking engagements. Regarding the art of Wing Chun that he has dedicated his life to, Sifu Lamb is available for private instruction.

Bruce Frantzis

http://www.energyarts.com/welcome-bruce-frantzis

Bruce Frantzis, Ph.D., is a Taoist Lineage Holder with over forty years of experience in Eastern healing systems. He is the first known Westerner to hold authentic lineages in Tai Chi Chuan, Baguazhang, Shing-yi Quan, and Taoist meditation. He has taught Taoist energy arts to more than 15,000 students. The foremost Western expert in two different styles of Tai Chi Chuan, he trained for over a decade in China has extensive experience in Zen, Tibetan Buddhism, yoga, kundalini, energy healing therapies. He teaches six powerful Qigong sets as well as Baguazhang, and Shing-yi Quan from the martial, health and meditation perspectives.

Carl Totton

http://www.drcarltotton.com

A practitioner of the internal martial arts for well over four decades, Dr. Totton, a licensed, Board-Certified Diplomate in School Neuropsychology (ABSNP), is a professor of psychology in both clinical and educational psychology. He works with a wide range of emotional and behavioral issues providing services that span from therapy for depression and grief counseling to parenting support, couples counseling and beyond. In a comfortable and supportive atmosphere, he offers a highly personalized approach tailored to each of his client's individual needs to help attain the personal growth they're striving for. "I work with adults, adolescents, and children."

Chun-Yi Lin

http://www.springforestqigong.com

Neil Kay, M.D., Prof. of Medicine at the Mayo Clinic College of Medicine in Rochester, MN., says this of Master Yi-Lin: "The way qigong is practiced and taught by Chun Yi-Lin is a very powerful approach to human health." Fluent in five Chinese languages, some as different from each other as French is from German, Chun Yi-Lin is a certified International Qigong Master and the creator of Spring Forest Qigong. Since coming to the United States in 1995, he has helped more than a quarter of a million people to learn about the powerful, healing benefits of Spring Forest Qigong. His vision is to have a healer in every family and a world without pain.

Hon K. Lee

www.sportsedgeacupuncture.com

Hon K. Lee, L.Ac., Dipl.OM, a Licensed, Board Certified Acupuncturist and Chinese herbalist, is owner of the Sports Edge Acupuncture Clinic, and also an adjunct professor at the Virginia University of Oriental Medicine. He is a Spring Forest Qigong Certified Instructor and Qigong Master.

Master Lee co-founded the Jow Ga Shaolin Institute, and is a disciple of both Jow Ga Kung Fu Grandmaster Chan Man Cheung and Shaolin Mizong Quan Grandmaster Lu Junhai. He also studied weaponry with Cha Style Grandmaster Chen Enyi, and earned a black belt in Shotokan Karate. He co-authored "Yang Style Tai Ji Quan: A Beginner's Guide."

A Marine combat veteran, he joined the CIA after active duty. His memoir "Paths Less Travelled of a Scholar Warrior (Spy) Teacher Healer," chronicles his adventures growing up in NYC's Chinatown, fighting in Vietnam, running CIA clandestine operations, apprenticing with martial arts masters, and studying Chinese medicine. All proceeds from his book go to charities that benefit combat veterans suffering from wounds of war.

Hong Liu

http://goo.gl/vE2U5

A world-renowned authority on natural healing and complementary health practices, Hong Liu is a living treasure in China and Hawaii. As a Western-trained, research-based physician, and a master of natural healing—the highest attainable standing in the centuries-old Chinese healing tradition—Master Hong has worked with the National Institutes of Health (NIH) and National Cancer Institutes (NCI) researching Chinese herbs that may have significant therapeutic benefit in adjunct cancer treatment. He is an adjunct professor with the University of Hawaii. The university has been a co-sponsor of Master's Asthma Humanitarian Event over the last four years and a Natural Healing Drug Rehab program for crystal methamphetamine addicts. Both have produced encouraging results.

Jerry Alan Johnson

International Institute of Medical Qigong

Professor of Medical Qigong Science and Philosophy and Director/Professor of Medical Qigong Therapy Dr. Johnson is licensed as a Doctor of Traditional Chinese Medicine (D.T.C.M.) in Beijing, China, by the People's Republic of China's Ministry of Health, and has served with national and international committees to promote and encourage the practice of Medical Qigong Therapy.

Having studied Chinese Energetic Medicine for more than forty-one years, he is recognized both in China and the West as America's leading authority on Medical Qigong Therapy. He is the Founder and Executive Director of the International Institute of Medical Qigong, in Monterey, California, and has designed several Medical Qigong programs which have been implemented into various T.C.M. Colleges and Medical Qigong Institutes throughout the United States,

Belgium, Bermuda, Brazil, Canada, Central America, England, France, Germany, Ireland, South Africa, and Sweden.

To date, Professor Johnson has presented many papers on clinical research utilizing Medical Qigong Therapy. He has also written and published over six Clinical Textbooks on the practice of Medical Qigong Therapy. These special textbooks are currently used in many T.C.M. Colleges and universities throughout the world for the purpose of studying Chinese Energetic Medicine.

Traditional Chinese Medicine (T.C.M.), focusing on Acupuncture, Herbology, Medical Qigong Therapy, Traumatology, and Chinese Massage. He interned as a Doctor of Medical Qigong Therapy, specializing in the treatment of cancer, tumors, and cysts, and in treating Atrophy Syndromes (kidney "wasting-away" diseases).

Jesse R. Brown

http://detroitwholisticcenter.com

Jesse R. Brown, N.D. is CEO of Detroit Wholistic Center (DWC) and Wholistic Training Institute (WTI), both located in the city of Detroit since their inception. Dr. Brown earned his Doctorate in Naturopathy and Master Herbalist certification through Trinity School of Natural Health. He holds certifications in several alternative health disciplines such as Colon Hydrotherapy, Iridology, Reflexology, and Nutrition, over a span of 30 plus years. Since 1987, Dr. Brown and his staff of 10 at Detroit Wholistic Center, have helped over 50,000 people to improve their health through weight loss, cleansing programs, natural herbs, supplements, and education. His passion for empowering others to take responsibility for their own health and mission to, "Train a Healer in Every Home," led him to open the Wholistic Training Institute in 1999. Both institutions are historic because, DWC is the city's oldest wholistic health center and WTI is the first and Detroit's only State-licensed school for natural health training. Certification programs at WTI cover nearly 100 courses and offer over 3200 hours of training in Naturopathy, Herbology, Homeopathy, and other emerging natural health studies.

John P. Painter

http://www.thegompa.com

Having contributed so much to the well-being and holistic health of society, honored by world health and peace organizations for humanitarian contributions, awarded by NASA for his research, and enjoying an international reputation for his expertise in the Chinese internal martial arts and law enforcement communities, these few words are ill-fitting to justify the tremendous amount of sweat-equity, Dr. Painter, Ph.D., ND, has invested in his work. Though he has specialized in naturopathic medicine with an emphasis in Chinese Acupressure and physiotherapy, he is famed for creating the American Rangers Law Enforcement Martial Training Institute, and teaching defensive tactics to military tactical trainers, FBI, DEA, and special police officers.

Jonathan B. Walker

http://www.qissagebodysystems.org

Dr. Walker, PhD., LPN, RMT, MHt, is an accomplished QiGong practitioner, he uses this traditional Chinese healing art, similar to acupressure, to address a wide range of health conditions from cancer rehabilitation to chronic health conditions such as arthritis. He incorporates the holistic practices of Tai Chi Quan and QiGong into exercise physiology, physical rehabilitation and general health maintenance. As a graduate of the Institute of Hypnotherapy, Walker has a specialty in Medical/Dental Hypnotherapy approved by the International Hypnosis Federation's Medical & Dental Division. He has also been board approved by the American Board of Hypnotherapy, The International Association of Counselors and Therapists and the International Medical & Dental Hypnotherapy Association. He recently completed training from Stanford University as a Master Trainer for Chronic Disease Self-Management programs, a self-efficacy program directed to help people who live with chronic diseases, improve the quality of their lives.

In April 2002, Walker received a Governor's Proclamation from New Jersey and in April 2003, he received a Joint Legislative Resolution from the New Jersey Senate and General Assembly in recognition of World Tai Chi & QiGong Day. He organized this local event in conjunction with the international celebration to increase public awareness about the holistic benefits of eastern health practices.

Walker was selected by the New Jersey Institute for Successful Aging, University of Medicine & Dentistry, School of Osteopathic Medicine to participate in a six-month research study to learn of the affects of Tai Chi on Alzheimer's patients.

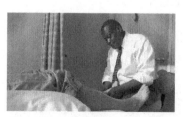

Joseph S. Acquah

http://www.taichidoc.com

A founding member of the clinical staff of the Osher Center, Joseph Acquah specializes in Asian medicine and Acupuncture, advocates and utilizes a three-pronged approach to providing preventive, chronic, and surgical treatment and care, and participates in all three departments of the Osher Center: Clinic, Education and Research. Additionally, he regularly teaches medical students at UCSF.

In 1995, Essence Magazine named Joseph as one of the top 100 alternative practitioners in the United States. With a master's degree in Clinical Psychology he is a nationally recognized Diplomate in Acupuncture (NCCAOM). He is the former Clinical Director and Internship Coordinator for the California Acupuncture College, served as an expert consultant for the State of California Acupuncture Examination Committee, and has taught at several colleges including Emperors College of Oriental Medicine, New England School of Acupuncture, and American College of Traditional Chinese Medicine. He was also an adjunct professor at Antioch University, as well as guest lecturing at Yo San University of Oriental Medicine and UCLA.

Dr. Acquah has practiced acupuncture for over 25 years and the Art of Tai Chi Chuan for 30 years.

Kam Yuen, D.C.

http://yuenmethod.com

Dr. Kam Yuen, DC, a former aerospace engineer, is noted for his expertise in Tai Chi Chuan and Qigong, as well as Feng Shui. According to the World Black Belt Organization he is a 'Living Legend.' He is also recognized as the legendary, 35th Generation Grandmaster of Shaolin Kung-Fu. Dr. Yuen was the consultant and stunt coordinator for the original television series Kung Fu, featuring the late David Carradine. He also played the roles of Wong Ti and Lin Wu in the series and was the double for Keye Luke, who played Master Po in the series.

Not resting on his laurels, however, for the last twenty years this retired grandmaster has taken his legendary status up several notches by always innovating and continuously pushing the envelope for the maximization of human potential physically, mentally, and spiritually. Taking wellness and everyday living to new levels he has successfully treated over 300,000 patients who were suffering from acute or chronic health conditions and life issues. Even well-known celebrities such as: Mrs. Martin Luther King, Steven Seagal, Chuck Norris, Stevie Wonder, Dick Gregory, Robert Deniro, Keith Carradine, Morgan Fairchild, Paula Abdul, Seal, Jack Canfield, Dan Millman, Louise Hay, Michael Beckwith, and others have consulted with him.

Many universities and centers for spiritual development have hosted Dr. Yuen, including Stanford, Kaiser Permanente, and The Deepak Chopra Center. His travels have taken him to chiropractic, naturopathic, and acupuncture schools on four continents: Europe, Canada, Brazil, Thailand, Hong Kong, China, Japan, and the Philippines. Grandmaster Yuen has appeared on the 'Jay Leno Show', plus he has been featured on other TV programs such as 'Hardcopy,' 'Extra', and 'Strange Universe.'

Using a methodology he synthesized from Taoist practices, his martial arts experience and chiropractic studies, Dr. Yuen has A worldwide keynote speaker, Dr. Kam Yuen is a consultant, author, seminar leader, teacher, life coach and healthcare expert of high regard. 6520 Platt Ave #611, West Hills, CA 91307

Ken Cohen

http://www.qigonghealing.com

Ken Cohen (Gao Han) is the Executive Director and founder of the Qigong Research & Practice

Center. He is a world-renowned health educator, China scholar, and Qigong GrandMaster with more than forty-five years experience. A former collaborator with Alan Watts, he is the author of the internationally acclaimed book The Way of Qigong: The Art and Science of Chinese Energy Healing (Ballantine), best-selling self-healing audio and video courses (Sounds True), and more than 200 journal articles. In 2003 Ken Cohen won the leading international award in energy medicine, the Alyce and Elmer Green Award for Innovation and Lifetime Achievement.

Ken Cohen's teachers have included some of the most highly respected Masters and Grandmasters in the world, including William C.C. Chen (Yang Style Taiji Quan), B.P. Chan (Chen Style Taiji Quan, Bagua Zhang, Xing Yi Quan, Qigong), Madame Gao Fu (Chen Style Taiji Quan and Hunyuan Primordial Qigong), Share K. Lew (Taoist External Qi Healing), Sunyata (Vedanta in the lineage of Ramana Maharshi), Swami Venkatesananda (Sivananda Yoga), and others. Ken was the principle apprentice to Dr. Huang Gengshi (Henry K.S. Wong, 1910-1999), acupuncturist and Taoist Abbot from China's sacred mountains. To advance his study of Comparative Religion and facilitate healing work in hospitals, prisons, and other places of service, Ken attended the New Seminary during the late 1980s and was ordained as an interfaith minister with an advanced degree in pastoral counseling (Master of Spiritual Therapy M.S.Th.). He also holds an honorary M.A. in Psychology and other academic honors.

Ko Wong

http://goo.gl/FIDtw

Master Ko Wong's exceptional skills gained him international recognition as an advanced practitioner of Qigong. He is exceptionally skilled at treating people with severe health conditions including cancer and heart disease. Master Ko Wong was officially recognized as a Qigong Healing Physician in 1986. Two years later, he was appointed Assistant Director of the Qigong Self-Control for Cancer Prevention and Treatment Association of the China Cancer Research Foundation. For over thirty years, Master Ko has used natural Chi treatment to assist patients afflicted with illnesses ranging from cancer to migraine headaches. He also creates individualized restorative programs for patients with chronic health conditions. In 1995, Master Ko brought his teachings to the United States when he opened a clinic in San Francisco, California.

Michael Tse

http://www.londonqigong.net

Michael Tse is one of the most well-known teachers of Qigong, Chinese Martial Arts and Chinese Culture in the west. Through the loyalty to his teachers and hard work and dedication, he has built up a strong following of students all around the world. For several years, he studied Qigong healing—sometimes actually staying in her home for several weeks at a time—with Grandmaster Yang Meijun, who was the 27th generation holder of the Kunlun Dayan Qigong skill. Accordingly, she was the best and whose internal skill was very high-level. Under her guidance he learned Qigong healing and diagnosis, which he uses with his patients. Michael Tse has a great *wealth* of experience in Qigong, Chinese Martial Arts, and Chinese Philosophy.

Ming-Tong Gu

http://www.chicenter.com

Ming-Tong Gu is an internationally recognized teacher and healer who received his training from a variety of Grandmasters in China and at the world's largest Qigong hospital. This "medicine-less" hospital, Zhineng Qigong Center, has treated over 200,000 patients, with over 185 different illnesses, and with a 95% effective improvement rate. He is the founder of The Chi Center and Wisdom Healing Foundation and has taught Qigong to thousands of people in the USA, China, and Europe.

Grandmaster Nan Lu is the country's foremost spiritual leader, practitioner and teacher of traditional Chinese medicine (TCM) because of his dedication to preserving ancient lineage knowledge of TCM and Qigong not found in textbooks. As a longtime student of exceptional Chinese masters, Grandmaster Lu holds and preserves ancient lineage knowledge that has been passed to him without book learning.

His medical knowledge of meridians, the body's energy system, comes from Grandmaster Xi-hua Xu, Taoist philosophy professor and remote viewing expert whose healing skills have helped officials at the highest levels of the Chinese government. This unique Qigong master also transmitted the Spirit of Taiji to Grandmaster Lu whose internal martial arts expertise comes from one of the most respected martial artists in Chinese history, Grandmaster Wan Laisheng.

Grandmaster Lu has the unique gift of cross-cultural communications and can interpret essential, timeless spiritual and healing truths with clarity, depth, compassion and humor. To share his wisdom, he founded the nonprofit educational organization, Traditional Chinese Medicine World Foundation, where programs such as The Dragon's Way® Weight Loss and Stress Management Program and Breast Cancer Prevention Project today help tens of thousands of individuals. In Tao of Healing, his private practice, Grandmaster Lu guides patients as well as students of his Wu Ming Qigong School to understand the profound impact of consciousness on true healing through Taoist philosophy and Chinese medicine modalities.

He also selectively shares advanced healing techniques in his LifeForce: Tao of Medical Qigong training program. For more information: www.taoofhealing.com, www.tcmworld.org, www.breastcancer.com

Roger Jahnke, O.M.D.
http://IIQTC.org
http://FeelTheQi.com
http:TaiChiEasy.org

With thirty years of clinical practice as a physician of acupuncture and Traditional Chinese Medicine Dr. Jahnke has emerged as a key spokesperson for *Tai Chi (Taiji)* and *Qigong (Chi Kung)* and is a master teacher of these arts. With 9 research trips to China's universities, hospitals, temples and sacred mountain sites, he has distilled the essence of Qi cultivation in his two widely revered books *The Healer Within* and *The Healing Promise of Qi*. He has dedicated his professional life to sharing the empowerment based healing traditions of ancient China in accessible, easy to practice formats. Dr Jahnke is the director and chief instructor of the Institute of Integral Qigong and Tai Chi (IIQTC); a world renowned training and research institute in Santa Barbara, California that has trained 1000 Teachers and Practice Leaders and produced innovative research. He is the cofounder and recent chairperson of the National Qigong Association (NQA). To empower those less likely to have access to the benefits of Qigong and Tai Chi, Dr Jahnke and colleagues founded The Healer Within

Foundation which trains Tai Chi Easy Practice Leaders who empower underserved populations to eliminate the necessity to treat preventable chronic diseases by preventing them instead. He is the translator/editor of the clinical chapters of the first English language edition of *Chinese Medical Qigong* -- the official Qigong text used in the medical schools of China.

Teresa Yeung

www.TheSeventhHappiness.com

Master Teresa Yeung is a highly respected generational master of Chi Gong. She became the sole successor of internationally acclaimed grandmaster Weizhoa Wu Qigong lineage. She continues to evolve his teachings, while developing a new level of Qigong that balances her students' emotional and spiritual bodies. She also explores the ways of connecting to the 'unknown' mysteries of the universe through the use of the traditional knowledge of Master Wu.

Her popular instructors' programs and modified traditional techniques were created to suit the North American mindset, and in doing so, she has been attracting more students who wish to become instructors to spread her mission and continue on her tradition for generations to come.

In 2014, she became the Founder, President and Head Instructor of the Seventh Happiness™ School of Chi Gong - recognized and approved by the Ministry of Employment and Social Development.

Master Teresa teaches all across North America and many of the programs she currently offers include:

Medical Chi Gong Certification Program for Healthcare

Professionals and Therapists:

- General Instructors Program
- Ancient Fa Chi Healing Program for General Practitioners
- Ancient Fa Chi Healing Program for Acupuncturists
- Chi Gong for Yoga Instructors
- Explaining Energy Medicine
- Chi Gong for Office
- Chair Chi Gong

Master Teresa received the Unity Congress of the World Organization of Natural Medicine in Qigong in 2006 and Award of Merit for Outstanding People of the 20th Century.

Tom Tam

http://www.tomtam.com

As a writer, poet, and healer that came to the US as a political refugee in 1975, Tom Tam is a licensed acupuncturist in the state of Massachusetts and has practiced acupuncture in Chinatown, Boston for 25 years where he also taught Tai Chi, and Chi Gong healing with great success

Tu Jin-Sheng

http://MasterTu.com

With 60,000 followers worldwide including students in Malaysia, Japan, Italy, France, Canada, and the United States, Tu Jin-Sheng is a world renown master of Qigong and Chinese medicine. He is recognized as a Professor in medical societies in Taiwan, Japan, Canada and the U.S.A., having graduated from the prestigious Teachers Physical College of Taiwan with a degree in martial arts and a master's in Traditional Chinese Medicine. Tu is also a master painter and musician. He has been covered in Kung Fu Magazine, Playboy, Weekly World News, Ripley's Believe it or Not, National Geographic and England BBC.

It is widely known that and positively proven that Tu's popular Qigong can delay old age and prevent diseases, increase energy and vitality, make muscles and bones stronger, reduce arterial blockage, cholesterol levels, diabetes, allergies and ear problems. Additionally, of course, it can greatly enhance sexual performance. According to Grandmaster Tu, this method will increase the sperm count and boost male hormone levels in a way that is much more natural and better than taking drugs like Viagra or steroids.

Wong Kew Kit

http://www.shaolin.org

Receiving the "Qigong Master of the Year" award at the Second World Congress on Qigong held in San Francisco in November 1997, Wong Kew Kit is the 4th generation successor from the Shaolin Monastery of China. In addition, he is a bestselling author, healer, and beloved teacher to thousands worldwide, highly skilled in Chi Kung, Zen, and the martial arts of Shaolin Kung Fu, and Tai Chi Chuan. Additionally, he holds an honors degree in humanities, and is one of the very few masters who speaks excellent English.

Yuan-Ming Zhang

http://www.qigongmaster.com

Grandmaster Yuanming Zhang was born into a traditional martial arts family in Sichuan province in 1963. His entire life has been devoted to Internal Kung Fu and Traditional Chinese Medicine. He traces his lineage through renowned Zhang family ancestors.

For seventeen generations, Grandmaster Zhang's ancestors have studied, nurtured and refined traditional practices, acquiring knowledge for improving health and longevity. By the age of three, he showed a special gift for these practices, and was singled out for early instruction in calligraphy, martial arts, meditation and qigong. Grandmaster Zhang went on to study with twenty-four different masters and hermits, developing a broad, inclusive background in the traditional arts of Internal Kung Fu, Chinese Medicine, Acupressure Massage, Medical Qigong, Daoism and Tibetan Buddhism.

Grandmaster Zhang has earned international recognition for his expertise in a variety of martial arts systems, including Chenzhen, Emei, Wudang, and Shaolin. Among his teachers are Lu Zijian, Li Ziming, Yin Yi, Zhong Fanghan, and Zhang Wenguang. Since 1992, he has devoted himself to bringing these traditional arts to the Western world. He has been a Consultant to the United Nations Qigong Society.

Yang Jwing-Ming

http://ymaa.com

Well-known, highly accomplished and widely traveled, Dr. Yang has had the privilege to share his extensive knowledge with the world for over three (3) decades. This esteemed professional travels between Yang's Martial Arts Association (YMAA) International Branch and Provisional schools presenting lectures and seminars on Chinese martial arts and Qigong. He has visited Argentina, Austria, Barbados, Botswana, Belgium, Bermuda, Canada, China, Chile, England, Egypt, France, Germany, Holland, Hungary, Iran, Ireland, Italy, Latvia, Mexico, Poland, Portugal, Qatar, Saudi

Arabia, Spain, South Africa, Switzerland, and Venezuela. Dr. Yang has published over 35 books and more than 50 videos on the martial arts and Qigong.

Yun-Chung Chiang,

http://www.wenwuschool.com

In 1973, Dr. Chiang opened the Chung Hua (Chinese) Clinic within Wen Wu School. Treatments include acupuncture and herbal medicine. The clinic is also managed by Dr. Erlene Chiang. Since its opening, the clinic has treated over 3,000 patients.

There are numerous excellent and highly rated Qigong doctors and internal martial arts masters spread throughout the world. If none of the above masters are in your vacinity, and you have a desire to check your progress, there may be masters or qualified top students of masters who are well-equipped at helping you to achieve results. Google the word **Qigong Masters** in order to ascertain if there are masters in or near your vacinity that you may visit.

References

1. Larkey L, Jahnke R, Etnier J, Gonzalez J. Meditative movement as a category of exercise: Implications for research. Journal of Physical Activity & Health. 2009;6:230–238. [PubMed]

2. Jahnke R. The Healing Promise of Qi: Creating Extraordinary Wellness through Qigong and Tai Chi. Chicago, IL: Contemporary Books; 2002.

27. Chen K, Yeung R. A review of qigong therapy for cancer treatment. Journal of International Society of Life Information Science. 2002;20:532–542.

28. Cheung BMY, Lo JLF, Fong DYT, et al. Randomized controlled trial of qigong in the treatment of mild essential hypertension. Journal of Human Hypertension. 2005;19:697–704. [PubMed]

29. Lee MS, Jeong SM, Kim YK, et al. Qi-training enhances respiratory burst function and adhesive capacity of neutrophils in young adults: A preliminary study. Am J Chin Med. 2003;31:141–148. [PubMed]

30. Faber MJ, Bosscher RJ, Chin A Paw MJ, van Wieringen PC. Effects of exercise programs on falls and mobility in frail and pre-frail older adults: A multicenter randomized controlled trial. Archives of Physical Medicine & Rehabilitation. 2006;87:885–896. [PubMed]

31. Fransen M, Nairn L, Winstanley J, Lam P, Edmonds J. Physical activity for osteoarthritis management: A randomized controlled clinical trial evaluating hydrotherapy or tai chi classes. Arthritis & Rheumatism. 2007;57:407–414. [PubMed]

32. Greenspan AI, Wolf SL, Kelley ME, O'Grady M. Tai chi and perceived health status in older adults who are transitionally frail: A randomized controlled trial. Phys Ther. 2007;87:525–535. [PubMed]

33. Li F, Fisher KJ, Harmer P, Shirai M. A simpler eight-form easy tai chi for elderly adults. J Aging Phys Activity. 2003;11:206–18.

34. Yeh GY, Wood MJ, Lorell BH, et al. Effects of tai chi mind-body

movement therapy on functional status and exercise capacity in patients with chronic heart failure: A randomized controlled trial.[see comment] American Journal of Medicine. 2004;117:541–8. [PubMed]

35. Chodzko-Zajko W, Jahnke R. Working Group. National expert meeting on qi gong and tai chi: Consensus report. Urbana, Il: University of Illinois at Urbana-Champaign; Nov, 2005. Available from: http://healerwithinfoundation.org/National_Expert_Meeting/

Additional References

http://fitlife.tv/6-super-mushrooms-to-rock-your-world_original/#sthash.C3Qy76Qk.dpuf

http://www.naturalnews.com/049638_reishi_mushroom_cancer_treatment_natural_medicine.html#ixzz3mrUuRBfM

http://shadowheartandsouloftheblackrose.ning.com/group/the-shroom-room/forum/topics/reishi-lingzhi-mushroom-ganoderma-lucidum

http://www.creationtips.com/bitter_sweet_water.html

http://articles.mercola.com/sites/articles/archive/2014/06/30/ginger-health-benefits.aspx

http://www.rense.com/general63/DISEASE.HTM

The Book on Internal STRESS Release is sponsored by

Magic 10 Nano-Silver is an all-natural liquid drink that is extremely beneficial to your health. Just several of the many benefits provided are: it is an anti-viral, anti-bacterial, and anti-microbial, **ALL-IN-ONE**.

Because of nano-silver's validity, the National Aeronautics and Space Administration (NASA) recently made the decision to adopt Russia's method of purifying its water after coming to the realization that adding ionized silver to water is easier, more effective, and much more efficient than adding iodine. Also, many hospitals keep it handy in burn units. It also assists in helping people with ailments such as eye infections, gum disease, sore throat, the common cold, intestinal problems, bladder and urinary tract infection (UTI), athlete's foot, fungal infections, and---for females---yeast infections.

Some external applications that this nano-silver may assist in helping include: Cuts, Grazes, Burns, Dandruff, Itchy Scalp, ringworm, boils, cold sores, acne and warts.

Even skin conditions like Psoriasis and Eczema may benefit from frequent application.

Order yours at **www.More.sh/Magic10-NanoSilver** or Scan the QR Code on the right to replace a host of other products you may be using, thereby helping you to save time and potentially hundreds to thousands of dollars annually.

Coach Melvin with his Internal Martial Arts teacher, the late Liang, Qiang-Ya

Made in the USA
Charleston, SC
10 November 2016